THE
PILLARS
OF AN
ELITE
SALES
CAREER

BENJAMIN RIALL

First edition 2020

Book editing by Jasmin Naim
Book proofreading by Alex Horton
Book cover design by Mary Ann Smith
Book interior design by KUHN Design Group
Book illustrations by Dave Mohammed

ISBN 978-1-8383411-0-7 (paperback)
ISBN 978-1-8383411-1-4 (e-book)

Published by Elite Sales Careers Ltd
www.elitesalescareers.com

CONTENTS

CHAPTER 1

HOW I UNCOVERED THE PILLARS

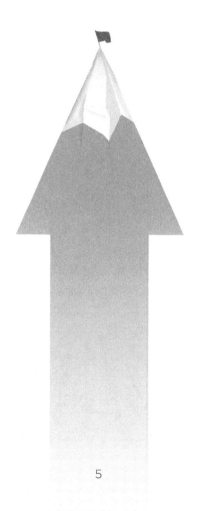

For some, sales is a lifestyle choice, while for others it is just a job.

Few careers have such a clear correlation between what you get paid and what you produce.

In a good month, when you crush your target, bring in the deals and receive the praise of the company, your success resembles what everyone works so hard for. Based on what you sell and how much of it, there can often be an impressive paycheque to look forward to. Perhaps that might be enough money to treat yourself to an expensive shopping trip, a long weekend or even a deposit on a house.

Yes, commission payments get that big!

In a bad month, if you miss your target and stray from where you should be, life can be pretty abysmal. The results include the feeling of failure, the cold shoulder from colleagues who expect better of you, and facing the feared slippery slope. Not to mention an unappealing paycheque.

In some sales jobs more than 70%, even up to 100%, of the money is from commission, so missing your target can be the difference between eating or not that month.

WHAT IS THE SLIPPERY SLOPE?

In sales we are both measured by, and rewarded on, our performance. If we continue to underperform, week by week, month by month, the pressure from management increases. As someone slides down the slippery slope, fear strikes; the end of that slope is the door, and by the door I mean getting fired. This means being told to pack up your things, hand in company property, leave and never return. Yes, it can be that harsh!

The problem with the slippery slope is not just the inevitability of being fired and the fear of running into financial issues, the problem is psychological. In sales it's essential to stay in a positive place, because this positivity is what we portray to others and people buy into that. If we are under pressure to perform, it can create a negative energy within us, and as that pressure increases, remaining positive becomes harder. The speed with which we might then slide down the slippery slope only accelerates.

Yet for some this brings out the fight in us, refusing to give up, refusing to accept the shame of failure. We dig deep, ignore the negative pressure, do what it takes to perform and rise from the ashes. Some will even rise as high as the top of the sales ranks with a hell of a story to share. This is sales.

Most sales professionals just get by; they have their good months, they have their bad. To be average in sales, as most are, affords a modest lifestyle.

To put that in context, let's assess the average global pay of salespeople, which is a difficult task as governments collect and categorise this information in different ways and there are varying levels of public exposure. The U.S. Government's Bureau of Labor Statistics[1] provides the most reliable illustration of this point. To help interpret their 2018 statistics, I took the median pay of all salespeople, excluding retail salespeople, and then weighted them by industry, to give an accurate overall representation.

Table 1: Median pay of salespeople in the U.S., adjusted for proportion in each industry

INDUSTRY	NO. PEOPLE	MEDIAN WAGE	WEIGHTING	MONETARY VALUE
Insurance	393,830	$67,890.00	0.09	$6,185.40
Finserv	415,890	$98,770.00	0.10	$9,502.91
Travel agents	69,480	$42,720. 00	0.02	$686.66
Services	1,033,820	$64,860.00	0.24	$15,512.25
Manuf/Wholesale/ Scientific—technical	312,980	$91,830.00	0.07	$6,648.97

INDUSTRY	NO. PEOPLE	MEDIAN WAGE	WEIGHTING	MONETARY VALUE
Manuf/Wholesale/ Scientific—non technical	1,350,180	$69,480.00	0.31	$21,702.23
Demonstrators	81,250	$33,260.00	0.02	$625.17
Real estate brokers	40,320	$78,940.00	0.01	$736.33
Real estate agents	156,760	$61,720.00	0.04	$2,238.28
Sales engineers	65,720	$108,610.00	0.02	$1,651.28
Telemarketers	164,160	$28,550.00	0.04	$1,084.24
Door to door	9,430	$34,120.00	0.00	$74.43
Sales other	95,690	$40,480.00	0.02	$896.11
Advertising	133,110	$63,360.00	0.03	$1,951.10
	4,322,620	$63,185.00		$69,495.35
				Average pay

(Source: Author, based on USA Bureau of Labor stastics)

Table 1 shows us that the median pay for salespeople in the U.S. is $69,495, after the relative proportion of individuals working in each industry is accounted for. Naturally, the median pay for salespeople differs from country to country, but this discussion will use the example of the U.S. Wherever you are based, you must ask yourself this important question: why just be average in a profession like sales? Think of the pressure you put yourself through, the constant battle to bring in the deals and the strength of the internal competition. If average is all you are aiming for, there are easier ways to make the equivalent of $69,495 a year!

Then think of the Elite. Picture their immaculate hair, sharp dress sense, a glow in their eye, a bounce in their step as they walk, standing proud and firm. When they speak, their voice commands you to listen, and when you speak it's as if they can listen beyond your words to the very meaning of your presence. Month after month, they crush their number and maintain the utmost respect from their colleagues. Other salespeople look up to them and aspire one day to become like them.

So, how much do the Elite earn per year?

Once again this is not a straightforward answer for the same reasons it is difficult to calculate the average pay of a salesperson. In 2011 the respected publication, Forbes, explored this topic, and discovered that enterprise software salespeople are amongst the highest paid of all salespeople and the top percentile earn over $200,000 per year.[2] The rare few even break through $1m in a tax year.

A common perception is that you'd have to be a CEO or high-ranking banker to earn that sort of money.[3] The Elite in sales are the exception, and this is their reality. Life can get interesting with that income.

Yet the journey to becoming an Elite salesperson is not well documented compared to becoming successful in other well-paid professions, such as law, medicine, accountancy and the like. There are plenty of well-regarded books and sales training courses on methodology, but almost nothing on how to build a career to reach the top of the sales profession. It seems that you've got to just kind of figure it out.

Why should this be a mystery? Surely there is a common path to becoming Elite in sales? If tens, or maybe even hundreds, of thousands, of people have achieved this in modern history, then why can't we? During my journey building my career as a sales professional, I'm proud to say I made it to the Elite. Along the way I made some interesting observations about the different ways people made it to the top of the profession, and plenty more on why some people did not.

Success did not come easy to me and I wasn't born into wealth, yet I've visualised achieving a great deal of success in my life for as long as I can remember. At 12 years old I experienced the first sensation of closing a sale, when a kid mistook me for someone else and asked if I had any Games Workshop models for sale, as they were popular at the time. In my garage at home sat a small army of figurines, ready for battle. I took the initiative and replied: '*Yes, I live around the corner, let's go!*'

With my first taste of sales and £50 in my pocket, as a 12-year-old at the turn of the millennium, I felt like I had closed a multi-million dollar deal as an Elite salesperson! Little did I know then that sales could be a career.

Throughout my teenage years I earnt myself an image of Del Boy, a character from a famous British comedy, *Only Fools and Horses*. Sports shoes imported from China, electronics, push-bikes, DVDs: whatever I could get my hands on, I found a way and I made a profit—most of the time at least. My most effective sales channels were:

- eBay
- direct to friends

- to friends of friends
- family friends
- out the back of my car at car boot sales

Whatever, however, I was there! My love of boxing and on/off training spent in the local famous boxing gym, Essex Road in Basingstoke, only fuelled my image.

When secondary school and college finished, at the age of 18 it was time to get serious. I had to move on from my hustling days and become the businessman I always dreamed of being, inspired by famous English entrepreneurs such as Alan Sugar, Richard Branson, Peter Jones, Duncan Bannatyne and many more. Rather than going to university, my first business, an unusual venture, was born.

GHD hair straighteners were big! Everyone was talking about them, but where I grew up everyone spoke mostly about the price tag. On eBay I discovered a hair straightener claiming to be as good, but half the price. I bought a few, tested them at the local hair salons and all the proof I needed was there. Branding doesn't mean a product is the best in the market. However, a brand wasn't just going to give an 18-year-old distribution rights, so I needed to show that I had a network.

What goes with hair straighteners? Hairbrushes! Town to town, salon to salon all across the English county of Hampshire, I sold hairbrushes for commission only four days a week, alongside three days a week of construction work, digging holes to fund fuel for my car, and beer. Slowly, slowly things took shape... but then I realised that I really didn't care about this market. What the hell was I doing? The only reason for selling hair straighteners was because there was more profit in them than in hairbrushes. My motivation depleted, I gritted my teeth and called it a day.

At first this knocked my confidence, and it was difficult to accept failure. A wild six months in Puerto Banus, Marbella, Spain put my mind at ease and mentally prepared me for the next venture.

Throughout my young teen years I often remember the treat of heading to the local video store with a friend, picking up a couple of gory 18-certificate films that we shouldn't have been allowed to watch and having the best nights in. It's an experience younger generations will never have. Then the rise of online streaming services made it too hard for the local video store to make a profit, and led to their closure, which was micro-scale compared to the closure of the video rental giant Blockbuster in 2010.[4]

At that point, digital was the future, disruption was to become the norm and the possibilities were endless. I had to get involved, which led me to join a start-up website development company, with the intention of setting up sales and marketing campaigns to generate new business, again for commission only.

Envious of my friends' wild university stories, I decided that I should no longer miss out and enrolled at Bournemouth University to study Business Enterprise, with a part-time job selling websites. After three months I had missed almost all of my lectures and maxed out three overdrafts in the student bars (impressive when it was £1 a drink!). I soon realised that I was only there to party and meet pretty girls, so I left. If I had left a week earlier, I would not have needed to pay for the year. An expensive mistake, yet the memories remain priceless!

By now I was convinced that my ticket to becoming a millionaire was to lead independent high-street retailers online, as e-commerce was fast emerging. However, an issue I soon encountered was that e-commerce created a stock management headache for independent retailers. When a product is sold online, from the shop or vice versa, the records do not sync, so I designed a solution to stitch together several software packages. One concern remained. Multiple systems stitched together sounded messy, and after some research it emerged that a few companies had already built such a solution. Time to go undercover.

The Managing Director of one of these companies was so impressed with my initiative that he offered direct mentorship, £20,000 basic salary and £50,000 OTE (On Target Earnings), as well as paying for my fuel (I was still digging holes for fuel and beer money). I was 20 years old, lacked skills, had no mentor and was on commission only. The decision to accept took little thought.

This is how I started my software sales career, even though at the time I had little understanding about the potential this career offered. Why would I?

This man taught me a lot about what it means to be a professional software salesperson. I was definitely rough around the edges at the start of this job. Driving down the motorway on the way to work, I remember feeling like I was drowning as I struggled to keep up with failure after failure. Had I encountered the slippery slope?

Eventually sales started to close and I could afford to rent a room in a shared house—and to stop digging holes for extra beer money. My run rate wasn't £50,000, it was closer to £35,000, which says more about my performance than the opportunity.

A voice called out to me, '*Are you earning £50k per year, working for a top-100 company? No? Then call Lead Forensics now!*' It was an ad on the radio, and I heard it twice more. Even though things had started to take shape in my job, I longed to be part of a company that had a stronger sales culture, so I got in touch. Three months later Paul Thomas, Managing Director of Lead Forensics, flew me in his private helicopter to the Manor House Chewton Glen in the English countryside for a winners' dinner, as I'd made it to the top of the sales board. Paul told me I was the only conversion from the ad and the ROI (return on investment) was exceptional.

Lead Forensics was a world away from my last role. There I had been the entire sales team, while at Lead Forensics, I was one of 15. During my time, this number grew to over 60. It opened my eyes to a proper sales culture that was arguably more cutthroat than others. If you did not perform in three months, then without question they would fire you. That never once scared me; it only motivated me.

Lead Forensics was where I became a successful salesperson, because the environment allowed me to thrive and learn from my peers. I learnt the importance of self-education, consistency in my sales performance and became sharp as a knife. It was also a lot of fun, since Paul created an office atmosphere that resembled the *Wolf of Wall Street*. It was a much tamer, more ethical and legal version of the film; the ambition and hunger of the sales team is what I refer to. When the film was first released, he took the entire sales team to the cinema to watch it. A couple of months later there was even a water slide in the office and the video of it went viral on Facebook!

On the same motorway a couple of years before where I had imagined I was drowning, I had an unfamiliar sensation. Cruising home in a brand-new sports car, tailored suit, buzzing after my best quarter that had placed me in the company's top three globally, I finally felt successful.

Even though my life had improved, it was not the case for 90% of my fellow salespeople. During the three plus years I spent at this company, I must have met several hundred people who walked through the door, filled with enthusiasm, picked up the phone to build their pipeline, but in just a few short months, were shown the door after failing to deliver.

What separated the top performers from everyone else?

The truth is that the best people listened to the calls of other top performers and also listened to their calls to identify ways to improve. This was something people did daily. In addition, top performers took training seriously. They read books, listened to audiobooks, took courses and did whatever else they could to improve. Then to tie it all together, they grafted. They had early starts and late finishes, daily. Whatever it took to achieve the sales numbers, they did, and when they achieved the results, they were rewarded for their efforts.

Quite frankly, those who failed did little or none of the above. Ok, it's simple to say it like that, and you can take into account those who had poor sales managers, or those people in unfortunate personal situations, and many more things. Yet the biggest reason was lack of commitment and focus. Sales can be harsh, particularly when you are starting out. No one said this would be easy.

Having broken through this stage and on an upward progression, my income increased year on year. I set my sights on breaking the £100,000 threshold.

I found myself musing on the fresh sea air blowing through my hair, the soft sand between my toes and being surrounded by my closest childhood friends. The thought would not escape my mind, because what's the point in financial success if you don't have a lifestyle to match it? It was on this beach in Surfers Paradise, Australia, celebrating a big year, that I decided that I needed to combine lifestyle and career. As fun as it was working at Lead Forensics, I lived in the small city of Portsmouth on the English south coast and believed that it had little to offer an adventurous and ambitious young man.

London seemed to be one of the most exciting cities in the world, as well as being the Europe, Middle East and Africa (EMEA) headquarters of Salesforce. This trailblazing company had been named Forbes No.1 innovative company four years in a row at the time. In addition, their software sales jobs ranked as one of the highest paying in the world. To join Salesforce became my mission, since there I could achieve many of my goals.

To commit to the change, I left Lead Forensics right away and prepared my move to London. There was no plan B; it was Salesforce or nothing.

After a hard three months and three attempts, I finally landed my dream job. Never had I been so overwhelmed or driven to succeed. This was my opportunity to achieve my financial ambitions and live in my dream city. My focus became more relentless than ever and my life more fun than I could initially comprehend.

Salesforce is a large company with many products, and the core of what they do is to centralise customer data and provide functionality for different parts of an organisation to effectively communicate with their customers at scale. A few of these divisions are Sales Cloud (flagship product), Service Cloud, and Marketing Cloud. I had secured a role in the Marketing Cloud and my responsibility was to launch a new adtech product and co-sell with the wider organisation.

When I joined Lead Forensics, they showed me my desk, gave me a script, instructed me to listen into other salespeople's calls, gave me my sales target and a pat on the back. Salesforce flew me to San Francisco for a week, gave me exceptional training, endless evenings of fun, a room in a 5* hotel and the opportunity to meet over 50 people from all corners of the world, who had also just joined the company. It filled every ounce of my being with a passion for Salesforce and a transfer to San Francisco became my three-year goal.

The calibre of the people I met was remarkable, as Salesforce only hires the best. By the skin of my teeth I got in. Here I worked side by side with people I admired, both in terms of what they had achieved in their careers and how they operated. I shadowed every person I met and paid close attention to how they did what they did. I was amongst the best in the industry; now it was time to prove I deserved to be one of their peers.

Without hesitation, I led by example and closed a stream of deals from an effective sales process I had designed. Then I taught it to more than 30 salespeople across Europe, organised multiple sales campaigns and together we obliterated targets. My reputation grew across the EMEA organisation and finally I had broken the £100,000 earnings mark, closer to £200,000 in fact. The buzz lasted for months.

Along with some wise investments in property and stocks, I also rewarded myself with several treats, including a year's worth of long weekends around Europe, a fresh wardrobe, and a watch to mark my achievement.

For my next challenge I wanted to be responsible for a bigger and more complex product. Salesforce had acquired the leading data management solution, Krux, for $700m, which they rebranded to Salesforce DMP and which is probably in its fourth iteration by now. There I saw an opportunity, positioning myself for this step up and fighting to get my name ahead of others. In spite of my efforts, to my delight it emerged that they had already awarded me this promotion, without the need to put myself forward.

2017 felt like it had 730 days rather than 365! In fact, I could write a book in its own right on the subject, but to keep it brief, there were some tremendous highs and lows, not to mention endless uncertainty. It was a time of huge personal development and new career milestones, false promises and overall, an incredibly memorable time in my life.

To summarise a key moment, in the midst of one of the first seven-figure deals I led, after tireless work we had received a verbal agreement that the prospect wanted to go ahead. To our surprise, our champions at the prospect were outvoted by the board. This client was part of a global group; it was a shocking loss for both the prospect and us. Funnily enough, I got to know the account executive who won that deal from our main competitor and they were just as shocked as we were... They also believed that the prospect wanted Salesforce. Sales is not always black and white. Despite this, it wasn't a complete loss because I'd learnt an incredible amount.

After that I won a stream of DMP deals in a row, most notably a $600,000 deal secured in five weeks, and a deal just $7,000 shy of $1m. It still eats me up that I didn't break the seven-figure mark!

It was during this time that I discovered my passion for public speaking. Because of my specialism in data-driven advertising, Salesforce selected me to speak at events in London, Amsterdam, Copenhagen and Brussels to C-level audiences of over 100 people. The talks helped to create a buzz and generate pipeline for the wider team—a good sign that I had delivered value on the day. Best of all I loved every moment of it!

Some of the key difficulties we faced that year were because, after an acquisition, in this case Krux being acquired by Salesforce, it can become volatile between the two teams. On one hand it is business as usual, but on the other, priorities include integration of processes, company training for both parties, new hires, people leaving, and the list goes on. All of this takes a lot of time and becomes a distraction from selling.

Personally, one of the harder challenges I faced was that my patch changed three times in the financial year. Working 12-hour days, I learnt from anyone who would help, focussed on what was within my control and hustled hard, but ultimately the constant switching of my patches damaged my momentum too much. For the first time in my professional sales career I did not hit my yearly target, landing at near enough 70%. That said, I still achieved more than my OTE (On Target Earnings) as I focussed on three-year deals. Salesforce rewarded me with a promotion, where this time I was set up for success.

My reward was San Francisco, my three-year goal, locked in. The role was to run a broader portfolio of products, based in San Francisco, covering the whole of the West Coast to secure new logos in the travel and hospitality sector, covering businesses sized between 1,000 and 5,000 employees. Just as exciting, my OTE was £200,000 plus, which was there for the taking. I cannot tell you how excited I was. This was a long-term goal and I had achieved it.

But then things came screeching to a halt. No degree, no visa. The U.S.

government would not let me in, despite all I had achieved and the support of Salesforce. Three months of work had gone into making this happen from both sides, and disappointment would be an understatement. For the first time in my career, not having a university degree held me back. A very good friend of mine was also moving to San Francisco. He is a senior manager in recruitment, has a degree in zoology and there were no problems for him!

Believe it or not, despite my dreams being shattered, it was easy to accept. I asked myself, what would I do differently if I were to replay this scenario? First thought, I should have forged a degree... but no, no, no, let's keep it legal. I thought again and my answer was that I had done everything within my power and executed my plan to make this happen. There was nothing I would have changed in my approach. So, it was very easy to accept and the next day I handed in my notice. My heart was no longer in Salesforce.

AN UNEXPECTED TURN

Denied entry to the United States, I set an alternative course. Fresh white sand crunched between my toes, the sea breeze off the Atlantic blew through my hair. I felt the Caribbean vibes of Central America, and lived the mantra of 'go slow'. A hike up the volcano Acatenango to watch the roar of Fuego erupt through the night. Diving 20 metres underwater on a single breath and my strength, the bliss of meditation. Surfing waves taller than six feet to let nature guide me forward. Making friends from all corners of the world, including the turtles and sharks under the sea. Sailing between tiny white-beached tropical islands, with the best company I could wish for. Endless wild adventures in Colombia and living to tell the tale. Hikes up mountains 6,000ft high and climbing cliff faces. Never-ending parties in my No.1 favourite place in the world, Rio de Janeiro.

After ten years of graft, I briefly let go of the horns of the bull. It liberated me. Being in the heart of nature, experiencing the most beautiful sunsets and sunrises and disconnecting from the fast-paced world of sales for nine months gives you a lot of time to reflect.

Along my path I'd now met hundreds, maybe even over a thousand salespeople. I can tell you from experience, the vast majority of these people were unsuccessful in sales. OK, they might afford a modest lifestyle, but in terms of financial success they were only starting to tap into the potential this career has to offer.

My story is only micro-scale, so how big is the sales profession?

THE SIZE OF THE SALES PROFESSION

As of 2019, it is estimated that there were 90.2m professional salespeople in the world.

This number has been arrived at on the following basis:

- The U.S. census states that the estimated number of professional salespeople in the U.S. in 2019 was 4.3m, which excludes retail salespeople.[5] Arguably you could say some retail people are in sales, but the vast majority are order takers.

- According to the World Bank, there are approximately 165.9m employed people in the U.S.[6] and so, of those, 2.6% are in professional sales.[7]

- Also according to the World Bank, in 2019 the global workforce was approximately 3.46bn people.[8]

- Assuming the same 2.6% heuristic, there are in the region of 90.2m professional salespeople in the world, all other factors being equal.

The culture in the U.S. differs from others in many ways, however it gives us a rough idea of the size of the sales profession. I welcome challenges to these numbers if you believe there are better data sources to examine.

If we assume 5% of the 90.2m, then 4.5m sales professionals globally are in the Elite. In country GDP relative terms, that means there are 85.7m who have not yet tapped into the full potential this career has to offer.

What sets the Elite apart? The top percentile of earners, those in more advanced economically developed countries, make six figures every year and some even break into seven figures. The difference is how they built their careers.

Sales methodology is just one component of making it to the top. The most significant part is how you plan and progress your career.

No matter if you started at the very bottom of the ladder and worked to the top, transferred from one career to another, joined a graduate programme and progressed to a senior position, there are five very clear commonalities in what people have done and will do in their career to make it to the Elite. We'll call them the five pillars.

Rewind back to the younger me. If someone sat down with me to share these five pillars and taught me how I could build my career around them, my journey to becoming Elite might have been faster and less painful. Looking at the bigger picture, the impact on me may not matter that much, because fortunately I made it there in good time. What matters is the impact it would have on the 90% or more of people who try, but struggle, to achieve any real financial success. Imagine the difference in raising a family on £60,000 a year plus a partner's salary, compared with £150,000 a year plus a partner's salary? The level of education the parents could provide to their children, the safe environment to grow and flourish, the travel experiences to open their eyes, and the comfort of pleasant things. Imagine the economic difference this extra spending power would have.

Salespeople are my people. I am a salesperson and, in some form or another, I'll most likely continue to be a salesperson. The thought of a life without commission shakes me to the core! Upon my return to London after nine months of backpacking in Latin America, I considered continuing through Asia and settling in Australia for a while, but the idea for this book was unshakeable; I had to bring it to life. So, in the coffee shops of Brixton, Clapham and Shoreditch in London, I started. Since the writing was underway and I'd caught up with friends and loved ones, I thought I could explore Asia and write. I set off for Thailand.

Soon into my writing I realised that my experiences were narrow-minded. How can one person's opinion of what success looks like relate to all? What I had was an hypothesis, so I set myself a quest to interview 50 Elite salespeople from all over the world who earn more than £100,000 a year. To prove my theory amongst 90% of Elite salespeople, surely that would hold some weight?

The rationale for choosing £100,000:

1. This level of income will put you into the top percentile of income earners, as previously explained.

2. For over 20 years the pound was stronger than the dollar or euro. By using the historically highest value currency of the three most commonly used in sales, it sets a higher bar for the income threshold.[9]

3. It is a mental barrier to break through six figures.

Now, where to find the Elite on a global scale?

The sectors I first considered were financial services, property, recruitment, consulting and software. Yet this list quickly narrowed down the more I analysed the topic.

In the U.S., property salespeople can earn a fantastic living at the top end of the market, but in European countries it is not the same, as commissions are far lower. Therefore I dismissed property salespeople for the purposes of this study.

Salespeople who sell high-end consulting services constitute an interesting group and one that has global norms. However, often the people who sell these services are consultants themselves or directors of the business. Again, it made little sense to focus here.

Next, I seriously examined the area of recruitment. After consulting with various senior leaders in the industry, however, I concluded that, even though recruitment is part of the sales profession and the pillars relate, it is different.

Financial services has long held the crown of the highest-paid sales profession; in particular, those who sell investments, high-ticket insurance or other high-value products. Similar to the consulting profession, sales is often only an element of their job. In addition, the barriers to entry can be unusually high as a certain level of academic qualifications are required. So, although financial services sales is a strong contender financially, the high barriers to entry led to me to dismiss the sector from the research project.

Which led me to software sales. Tech has boomed year on year since the inception of the computer and constant innovation promises continued growth. Not only that, country to country, the operating model is more or less the same. Becoming a sales professional is far more accessible than other industries and the very top-paid people are often individual contributors rather than managers. That said, the very senior leaders are usually the highest paid. Therefore, I focussed on software sales.

However, conducting 50 recorded video interviews in remote locations in Asia was a challenge, so I returned to London.

You would have thought the next part of the story would be a step back into sales, but given the intense focus that sales requires, I feared this project would never be more than an idea. Instead, I founded SaaS Catalyst, a SaaS start-up consultancy, where I advised tech founders on their go-to-market strategies and supported them on execution. Half my time would be on the book, half my time consulting. I committed to bringing this to life.

Before I started contacting the 50 Elite salespeople to validate my hypothesis, I had to be clear about what it was. It was in summary:

1. To be in the heart of the action

2. To be an industry/product expert

3. To be a student of sales

4. To receive mentorship

5. To own their career path

6. To be fuelled by passion

Each of the above needs a bit of explanation, but don't worry—read on and you will see.

My goal was to have someone share their career story with me in the most natural way, and throughout the interview I would dig a little deeper on key points as they related to the hypothesis.

The 45-minute interview format was something like this:

1. A quick personal and professional introduction.

2. What led them to starting a career in sales?

3. Ask them to share their story, the successes, the failures and the key things they learnt *en route.*

4. Ask them to share one of their hardest losses in their career, be that a deal, promotion, missed target or whatever, and the lesson they learnt from that.

5. What are the top three things they would say to a salesperson at the start of their career, to accelerate their success?

6. Then I would share my hypothesis at the end of the interview and how I believed that related to the person's career, to see if they agreed.

Before the interview, I sent a study overview and a consent form for each subject to review and sign, which they all did.

The task of booking in 50 interviews was almost identical to building a sales pipeline. Fortunately, I had a head start, already having a mental list of some of the best and most interesting Elite salespeople I'd met throughout my career. When I wrote this list down, there were 80 names from companies such as Salesforce, Amazon, Adobe, Pega, Oracle, LinkedIn, Snowflake, Datadog, Braze, and Segment.

To be honest, when I started contacting people it was quite a nerve-wracking experience. Contacting people to say 'hey, can I interview you to hear your career story to validate a hypothesis I have on how people become Elite in sales?' is quite an uncomfortable experience. Whether or not this would succeed, I was prepared to put my hard-earned reputation on the line. Unsurprisingly, not everyone replied as fast as I thought they would and to my surprise, people I thought unlikely to respond, did.

Yet I forced these negative thoughts out of my mind, looked at the bigger picture and pushed ahead.

The format of the interview facilitated a natural open conversation as it allowed the person being interviewed to open up and reveal things they might not have expected to disclose. So much so that some reported it as a liberating experience.

After a few weeks, ten interviews were complete and all of them validated the hypothesis. As happy as I was, reality hit. This was an enormous task! Self-doubt kicked in, a sensation I hadn't been all that familiar with, yet starting this interesting path meant it would be something I would encounter many times.

With the help of referrals, I booked a flurry of interviews and the path to 20 was clear, so I pressed on. Proceeding to completing 20 interviews, one by one each validated the hypothesis. A new level of confidence fuelled me, in fact I felt I didn't need to do any more interviews. However, the goal was 50, so I had to press on.

By this point I had contacted all the people on my list and it was clear that I needed to expand my search. I started a LinkedIn campaign, prospecting for one to two hours every day.

To identify top people I looked into the leading tech companies selling into enterprise and identified people on each team with a sound track record. In addition to digging further into the companies mentioned above, I targeted people at companies such as SAP, IBM, UiPath, Sprinklr, Dataiku, Gong, Yext, Atlassian, SalesLoft, Alfresco, Exponea, Marketo, MongoDB, Kenshoo, Optimizely, Databricks, and many more.

Throughout my campaign I contacted over 600 successful enterprise salespeople internationally, including from the U.K., the U.S., Australia, Canada, Ireland, France, Slovakia, Germany, Spain, Italy, Denmark, the Netherlands, Belgium, Sweden, Norway, Portugal, Switzerland, Finland, Japan, India, Singapore,

China, Brazil, Mexico, and UAE. The sample had no geographical boundaries. The only thing that mattered was success.

Interview by interview, I validated the hypothesis. People shared their fascinating stories with me of how they built their careers, how they had overcome failures, what drove them to push on, some incredible win stories, ambition and excitement for the future. It was an honour, with no judgement on either side; the sole goal to see whether what I believed I had uncovered was true. My efforts paid off. Soon I broke through 30 interviews, then 35, and then 40. All 40 at this point had completely validated the hypothesis.

With the last 10 in sight, I continued to push on, reaching number 45 with the 50th lined up in the diary, so prospecting stopped. 46, 47, 48, 49 and then finally 50! After five months of hard work, based on my genuine motivation to help others navigate this complex yet very rewarding career, I had validated the hypothesis. Besides this, there were also a few additional discoveries made along the way that we will discuss in later chapters.

To restate the hypothesis, Elite salespeople build their careers by:

1. being in the heart of the action
2. being an industry/product expert
3. being a student of sales
4. engaging in mentorship
5. owning their career
6. being fuelled by passion

The sixth point, being fuelled by passion, is in fact not a separate pillar, because passion is fundamental to all the pillars. If you are not passionate about the space you are in, being an expert in that space or the product you sell, being a successful salesperson, directing your career to a successful place and surrounding yourself with people to help you grow, you won't do it. Passion flows in all the pillars.

You might ask whether the hypothesis isn't just another sales methodology? In fact it's a little different. A sales methodology is a process you learn and follow to obtain an expected result. There is little open for debate. What I have uncovered is a career structure, the *Pillars of an Elite Sales Career*. You develop the pillars over time.

The interesting thing about the pillars is that people don't generally start with them in mind when they begin their careers. Sometimes people make very smart decisions about the industries they work in, the products they sell, and how they develop and grow. Often it just happens; the right company comes along, exceptional people surround them and the rest falls into place.

After listening to 50 stories, it became apparent that the pillars can establish themselves in so many ways. The important part is to establish them. When this happens, it's nearly always at that point that the person achieves major sales success that catapults them into the Elite. Those who continue to develop the pillars, push their success to even greater heights. It is a continuous process, and the very best never stop developing.

So this is not another sales methodology; these are the *Pillars of an Elite Sales Career.*

Finally, when you establish the pillars, something special happens. The person stands out as an individual, rather than a corporate clone. People look for ways to be natural and authentic in sales, to build trust with their prospects and love what they do.

The answer is that, on establishing the pillars for yourself, you will naturally be yourself. This is the underlying principle, authenticity.

Sales is a career for those who dare to dream big and do what it takes to achieve that goal, no matter who you are and where you are from. You are in control of your destiny.

Throughout this book you will not only learn the *Pillars of an Elite Sales Career,* but hear stories of many others who have built and continue to build their careers on these principles, backed up with practical advice on how to implement them.

Do not expect this book to be a silver bullet. Nothing good happens in life without hard graft and experience. The closer you follow the principles within the pillars, the sooner you will achieve your milestones in the successful career you have in front of you and the sooner momentum will kick in, which with the right focus will carry you to wherever you aim to be.

This book is for everyone out there who wants to better themselves and is prepared to do what it takes to make their dreams a reality. Once I have helped a minimum of 100,000 salespeople to learn the pillars and guided them on their path to join the Elite in sales, I will have achieved what I set out to do.

This isn't about me, this about you.

CHAPTER 2

INTRODUCTION TO ELITE SALESPEOPLE

B efore we get to the Elite, let's address the elephant in the room, namely that the sales profession has long held a bad reputation. The commission-chasing, fast-talking, ego-obsessed, slicked-back, snake-oil purveying image is what most people think about when they hear the title salesperson. Why have any desire to be someone like that?

The vast majority of us will only ever deal with Business to Consumer (B2C) salespeople, so to the outside world they are the face of the profession. Which is the problem.

THE SALESPERSON CLICHÉ

1. Buying a new car is an exciting experience and for many it will probably be a used car, at least in our earlier years of life. What a scene that can be, walking onto a muddy piece of land, cars neatly parked in a line, auto parts scattered around and a wooden shack in the corner with a sign barely hanging on that reads, '*Hanks Used Cars*'.

Most people know what car they want to buy, but on entering these types of places you never quite know what you will get, or even less whether we can trust Hank. All Hank cares about is closing the deal and securing his commission.

Should you go on to buy a car, as you pull out of the lot, you may question the vehicle's longevity.

2. Some of us don't drive, so perhaps haven't met Hank. But you've probably met Jack, the estate/letting agent. Imagine waiting outside the house you are about to view and then up pulls a small white Mini Cooper, plastered with *'Bradshaw Letting Agents'*. A cigarette butt flies out the window, the door is flung open and out steps Jack, taking a deep breath, brushing the cigarette ash from his blazer. He slicks back his hair before taking a step towards you.

'Afternoon, here to check out this gaff?'

Throughout the viewing Jack will sell you the dream, forget your family's and friends' names, tell you how he has had five offers on this property this morning and that you must place a high bid to secure it. His lengthy list of lines goes on and on. Somehow this familiar scenario has become an unavoidable experience in our quest for finding somewhere new to live.

3. Finally, if you haven't met Hank or Jack, you've certainly met Gemma. You'll find a Gemma down any busy high street, particularly in the cities. As you walk at pace on your way to work or possibly taking a quick break for lunch, someone will interrupt this moment of thought. Perhaps they greet you with some wild hand signals, an unusual dance or even a cartwheel, for the lucky few. What do they want?

They want you to 'save the world' and donate £20 a month to whatever charity it is they are representing today. Most likely you'll at the very best say 'no thank you', only for them to pester you a little more.

To set the record straight, I've donated to charity for a long time. Most of my donations go towards charities such as Save the Children and those that support disadvantaged people. I'm a big believer in helping younger generations have a better start to life to help humanity progress.

But there is no denying it, Gemmas are highly annoying! There are more, but I'm sure you get the gist.

For those who work in these or similar professions, I mean no offence; many in these roles are helpful and professional. And if this offends you, you will need to toughen up if you plan to join the Elite!

So, we've defined the Elite and why the focus is on software sales, and we've also met the Hanks, Jacks and Gemmas of the world. It's time to meet the 50 Elite salespeople that I interviewed during the research project.

THE ELITE

Haig Hanessian

At ten years old, young Haig Hanessian would walk around large factories on the edge of Mexico City to learn the ropes of his family business. The most important thing his Grandpa taught him is that these machines are worthless unless you have sales. From that point, Haig wanted to be in every sales meeting with his Grandpa and Dad, and started his training.

Haig and his family value education, so he progressed through the academic system and majored in marketing. He took a broad approach to expand his knowledge of business and sales. As exciting as marketing is as a career path, he knew his heart was in sales and the lucrative income potential was a motivator.

First, he took a step into the construction industry to sell retaining walls. However, if you were his client, you would have mistaken him for an engineer. The knowledge he possessed of his products and industry was beyond that of his peers and he won the trust of his clients. This trust secured him deal after deal and the commission flowed.

Haig's level of expertise did not go unnoticed. A water treatment company at the time had achieved rapid growth in Mexico and sought additional technical salespeople to handle demand. With better pay and career prospects, he joined the organisation and it wasn't long before he became an expert in this space. Success soon followed.

Not long after, the insurance market boomed. With a population increase and new insurance products coming to market, demand was high and insurance salespeople cashed in. The earning potential attracted Haig, though not so much the commission-chasing salespeople he met, with no other desire than to help themselves. Haig took a novel approach. He focussed on how he could help his customers, not take from them.

Consider life insurance, for example. If you're a factory worker, on a low income and you injure yourself at work with little protection from your company, how will you support your family? Haig developed a portfolio of five insurance products, solely focussed on how he could help people, and his book of business skyrocketed. So did his working hours!

Whilst catching up with a friend from university, it wasn't Haig's work ethic that surprised his friend. What surprised him was the fact he had to work much harder for similar money than his friend, who was a salesperson for the restaurant table-booking app, OpenTable. They were about to launch in Mexico and, inspired by his friend's story, Haig put himself forward for the position, quickly securing it, given his impressive background.

The vision for OpenTable was for a restaurant's customers to book via an app, improving the experience on both sides. However, this was 2007 and in Mexico the smartphone revolution hadn't reached mass adoption. OpenTable was ahead of its time. Most people would have quit, but Haig changed strategy. He repositioned it as floor management software and quickly his sales numbers excelled.

Despite a moderately successful start, Haig didn't bring in what he had before in insurance, but fortunately successful salespeople are always in high demand. An insurance company that needed a sales leader to lead a team of 40 approached Haig directly. Despite his growing passion for software, this was too great a challenge and career progression opportunity to pass up. He joined the team.

One thing high-performing individual contributors often struggle with when stepping into leadership positions is that they must rely on others to deliver business to their same high standards. Haig faced this challenge. Again, he put in the graft to be the leader that his team needed. His wisdom and people skills immeasurably helped to advance his team's success and careers.

Once again Haig caught up with his old friend, who had by now achieved outstanding success in enterprise software sales. Both shared the war stories they'd acquired in sales. As before, this friend opened Haig's eyes to the potential of the software market. As an Enterprise Account Executive for SAP bringing in millions of dollars for the company and closing six- and seven-figure deals, the buzz he got from that was something Haig hadn't felt in his own career to this date. The commission pay-outs were sometimes large enough to buy a house. OpenTable wasn't even on the starting line in comparison. Managing an insurance sales team was not even close.

Haig, fuelled with excitement, asked how he could get involved. His friend was concerned that Haig was too far into his career to transition into enterprise software sales.

Challenge accepted!

Fast forward to Haig, chilling on a sun lounger in Hawaii, waves crashing on the beach, a mojito in hand, next to his wife and surrounded by friends.

This was the marker of success. Four to five years after Haig's friend had said it was too late for him, he was enjoying his fourth Presidents Club trip in a row at SAP after achieving tremendous success selling their expense management system, Concur.

Haig's journey to become an Elite salesperson was not an easy ride. At first he thought joining SAP was the challenge, but the challenge was in fact to learn the role and how to be effective.

SAP was one of the top five software companies in the world and offered its employees some of the best training money can buy. Haig fully invested himself in everything they offered so he could become more like one of the successful Enterprise salespeople who helped mentor him at SAP. His dedication to self-development, combined with his determined nature, played a significant role in his success.

The lessons we learn in the field are often the most valuable. Sometimes we get emotionally involved in a deal. Haig truly believed the transformation that he could bring one of his prospects would revolutionise their business and so did his champions in their organisation. But power struggles plagued this organisation, such that people's own agendas came before the future of the organisation. Step by step Haig and his team got closer to securing the 7-figure deal, but after 24 months of the same story, SAP management pulled the plug. He was incredibly disappointed, not by SAP, but at his prospect for investing so much energy into doing nothing, which would no doubt hit them hard further down the line.

Several years later this organisation was in the spotlight in the press; having failed to digitise, revenues declined, people were being laid off, and the organisation was on its way out.

Sometimes there are things we cannot control. The knockbacks are part of the journey. Haig thrived, and as painful as this experience had been, he learnt a significant amount and that's helped to shape the person he has become.

Haig Hanessian's sales career wisdom

1. Work harder than anyone else.

2. Develop yourself and stick to the methodology.

3. Seek mentors.

Mandy Smithson

Often in a film scene portraying early modern times, you'll see a young person on the streets selling newspapers, shouting out the news of the day. That's not quite how Mandy Smithson began her sales career, but instead she sold the ads in the Dutch newspapers that once used to dominate ad spend.

As we grow up, many think long and hard about their future careers. If you ever meet Mandy or have already had the pleasure of meeting her, you'll know straight away that she is very personable. Her energy comes from talking with others. Upon her graduation from university, she wanted a career where she could get out of the office, to meet and talk with people. Sales was her calling.

Mandy entered the media industry whilst major digital disruption was in full force. The problem with newspaper ads is that it's difficult to measure the return, yet long had it been one of the primary ways to advertise your business alongside T.V., radio and outdoor advertising. Throughout the 2000s, search engines such as Google, Bing, and Ask Jeeves were on the rise and long-standing publications were transitioning online. The ones that survived, that is.

Mandy quickly transitioned from selling newspaper print ads to digital ads. In the digital era, advertisers faced the challenge of having too much choice of where they could place their ads and, on the flipside, competition became even more fierce for publishers. The next innovation in the industry addressed this problem: programmatic advertising, which automates the buying and selling of digital ad space. Advertisers decide the audience they want to reach and how much they want to pay for those ads and the technology does the rest.

Mandy saw that this was a far more effective way for advertisers to deliver value and specialised in this fast-growth area, which was still in its infancy. What intrigued Mandy the most was the underlying technology components. There were a few of these: an ad server that stores the inventory (ad space) amongst other things; a DSP (Demand Side Platform) that buys the ads on the publication websites; and a DMP (Data Management Platform), which is where the advertiser decides who they want to target. DMPs are at the more advanced end of the spectrum.

DMPs are often the starting point for programmatic advertising. Once the advertiser has created their audience in the DMP, it then connects with one or multiple DSPs, which connect with publisher's ad servers to bid for ad space on their website. Finally, the ads are served upon completion of a 'trade'. It's a far more efficient way of buying digital ads and, as you can probably imagine, it changes the role of a salesperson within the publisher organisations.

Mandy was centre stage of the disruption that occurred in the media industry and rather than being afraid, she thrived. As much as she loved helping her clients achieve their goals, she loved the innovation and technology.

After selling programmatic campaigns to her clients for a short while and understanding the sector, Mandy decided that the best way forward was to sell the technology, particularly as it was a white-hot space. One of the earliest innovators in this sphere was a DMP called Bluekai, the tech giant Oracle later acquired. Given her background in the sector, she easily got the position at Oracle, which came with a much larger compensation.

It's a big step to change from selling ads to technology, even with sound technical knowledge. Fortunately Mandy had some fantastic mentors and dedicated herself to not only learning the technology in depth, but also how to be an effective technology salesperson. Step by step, Mandy excelled, and she was in the market at the right time. Clients instantly bought into her, impressed by her knowledge and passion. Oracle had made an excellent hire.

One of the most memorable sales opportunities in her career was at Oracle. For confidentiality reasons, I can't reveal the name of the brand, but what I can say is that it is an iconic sports fashion brand. During this sales engagement she had never been so focussed. This was a must-win logo. Enterprise sales is a team sport and Mandy rallied her team to secure this logo; her career had been building for precisely this moment. She executed Oracle's sales cycle flawlessly, responded in what felt like the most efficient way and built a great relationship with the client. The sales cycle was more than a year, and both sides had invested a significant amount.

It was down to the final two vendors when she finally received that phone call. 'Mandy, you've been amazing, but I'm sorry to say that we are going with Krux...'

A devastating defeat.

The team at Krux were also very good, but their technology was the next-generation platform and Bluekai just wasn't the right product, despite how effective Mandy was. Management didn't quite see it this way and she faced a hard time. Shortly after this episode, Salesforce, a major competitor of Oracle in the customer experience technology space, acquired Krux. If you can't beat them, join them.

The sales leader for Krux was in awe when he met Mandy. He admitted she really put them through their paces and that they had lost a few deals to her. With hard feelings put to one side for both parties, they offered Mandy an excellent package and eagerly awaited her decision. It wasn't much of a decision; it was absolutely the right move for both sides.

At Oracle, Mandy was one of several selling Bluekai in the Benelux region (Netherlands, Belgium and Luxembourg) to businesses small and large. At Salesforce she was now responsible for solely strategic accounts in both the Benelux region and the Nordics (Sweden, Denmark, Finland, Norway and Iceland). A dream patch, with the best product and a world-class team. Mandy was pumped to get started!

Krux is a complicated application and most struggled to learn it in depth. Mandy's previous experience sped things up and she worked closely with the technical team to learn all she could.

Salesforce provides its employees with a €5,000 annual personal development budget, although most do not take advantage of it. Mandy did; she attended courses such as the *7 Habits of Highly Successful People*, negotiation courses, and others. This improved her sales skills and performance. You can probably guess what happened next.

Mandy crushed it! She'd never been so prepared and the market never so ready. Enterprises were on a spending spree for DMPs and she had the best product, as well as being one of the best salespeople in that category. Again, for confidentiality reasons I can't repeat the name of the logos, but she secured some of the most recognisable brands as clients in her patch.

Mandy lives outside her comfort zone; she's a believer in the saying 'fake it till you make it'.

When Mandy isn't chasing innovation, adding value to her clients, and above all crushing her number, she lives a highly active life with her long-term boyfriend. They live just off the canal in Amsterdam, windsurf and run marathons. She has run three to date.

Just in her early thirties, Mandy's had an astronomical start to her career and I believe she's just getting warmed up.

─────────────── **Mandy Smithson's sales career wisdom** ───────────────

1. Be bold and just go for it. 'Fake it till you make it'.

2. Don't be afraid to fail and to learn from your mistakes.

3. Seek mentors and coaches that can help you develop.

Dan Czasznicki

How you start your career in sales has a big impact on how fast you progress and join the Elite. Dan Czasnicki, a young Englishman, is one of the few who got it right out of the gates.

Whilst growing up, he wasn't sure what he wanted to do with his career. What he knew was that he wanted to make a lot of money, undertake challenging work, and interact with clients rather than work in the back office.

Before his career started, he studied Communications at Oxford Brookes University, England. As graduation neared, now was the time to get serious. Several of his peers had secured graduate jobs, yet Dan was still unsure of what career path to pursue.

Dan's Father was a Finance Director at a software company and saw great potential in him as a salesperson, both from a career success point of view and job satisfaction. This planted the seed for Dan. He researched sales as a career and spoke with various friends to get their perspectives. Before long, he was 100% convinced this was the right path.

When Dan applied for graduate sales roles, he stood out. It wasn't because of his good grades or charming personality, although these helped; it was because of his focus. Most people who apply for entry-level sales roles rarely make the conscious decision to pursue a career in sales; they rather fall into it. In fact, some people who apply for sales roles don't really know what salespeople do. Dan was at the opposite end of the spectrum. Not only did he know that he wanted to pursue a career in sales, he knew that it had to be in big-ticket software sales selling into large businesses. From his research, this was where the big money was to be made.

After filling out what seemed like endless application forms and a constant wave of interviews, he came across Open Text. Something instantly clicked.

Open Text is a large, international, industry-leading Canadian software company and their core offering is Enterprise Information Management (EIM). They also provide a variety of complementary solutions that range from compliance to business process automation. Since their founding in 1991, they have focussed on large enterprises, fixing the growing problem of managing content and data. As both the volume of content and data in enterprises grew exponentially, so did Open Text.

Dan's application was for a Business Development Representative (BDR) role and his job would be to arrange meetings for the Enterprise Account Executives through cold calling, direct emails, LinkedIn outreaches, and following up with marketing leads. He had never done this before, but was excited about the challenge.

Instantly Open Text was impressed with his focus, work ethic, energy and charisma. After several interviews they offered him the role, which he more or less accepted on the spot.

A first sales role is rarely a walk in the park. This was no different for Dan. Fortunately, Open Text had a good training programme and the senior salespeople on the team were highly supportive of his development. When you pair that with hard work and focus, success follows.

What inspired Dan the most was witnessing senior salespeople secure large six-figure contracts, receive the admiration of their peers, and then be rewarded with commission that was sometimes higher than Dan's annual base salary. He knew that if he delivered in his role as a BDR, one day this could be him.

Several months into the role, Dan was booking a consistent number of meetings monthly and buildings a good name for himself. This pace of success continued and in his first full year, Dan overachieved his target.

As the second year began, Dan was eager to progress and become an Enterprise Account Executive, yet he knew it was a big jump. He discussed his ambition with his colleagues and received exceptional advice from one of the senior salespeople: *'Achieve your role now whilst aspiring and learning your next role.'*

That is exactly what he did. As he made his ambition known, some senior salespeople let Dan join the first meeting, to develop a better perspective of what happens next in the sales process. Working with several salespeople, he built a broad perspective of different industries, challenges, solutions and sales styles. As the year continued, some salespeople even let him run with smaller opportunities to close independently. Of course, they guided him in the background.

As year 2 came to a close, Dan's role was very different compared to the other BDRs. He had successfully achieved his role and learnt the next.

Now was the time to ask management for the Enterprise Account Executive role. He'd consistently delivered his target, established his knowledge on Open Text's complex offering and closed a number of small deals, Dan was ready. He approached management and positioned the idea. Initially they were hesitant— it was still a big jump! But as he'd shown excellent initiative and potential, they wanted to see him succeed and grow in the organisation. The only issue was that they didn't have a suitable role, so management asked Dan to give them a few days to try to figure something out.

Several days later, Open Text offered Dan a newly created role. It was too risky to give him a large 7-figure target closing multiple complex deals with large enterprises; instead they gave him a small £500,000 target securing business with mid-sized organisations. This section of the market hadn't really been a focus, so required some creative thinking. Without hesitation, Dan accepted and walked out of the meeting room with a smile ear to ear.

Dan had made the tough transition from BDR to Account Executive within the first three years of his sales career.

Year 1 he delivered 120% of his target, which truly firmed his place as an Account Executive and he was rewarded with the promotion he'd longed for, to join the Enterprise sales team. That also came with a £1,000,000 target—twice as big as his last.

Year 2, again he overdelivered his number and year 3 wasn't that much different.

Year 4 he'd once again been promoted, but this time to the most senior sales position in the team, managing the top 10–20 enterprise accounts in the business, with a target of £2,000,000. You can probably guess what happened next...

Dan's promotion to Account Executive had started out as 'doing Dan a favour' and he progressively became one of the most respected salespeople in the company.

Seven years had passed since he had joined as a graduate salesperson at Open Text and the technology had rapidly developed. Dan found himself increasingly involved in sales cycles that involved customer experience technology which helps large brands to personalise their digital marketing communications. Of all the use cases he worked on, customer experience technology excited him the most; he felt this is where the industry was headed. Open Text had a good offering in this area, although it wasn't the leading provider.

Dan took a step back to analyse his career trajectory. He felt he'd achieved all he could at Open Text and now was the time to move on. Rather than approach recruiters, like most, he'd made a short list of four leading customer experience technology vendors that he'd decided he'd like to work for. With all four he secured an interview, but there was one in particular that topped his list: Adobe.

Adobe is a global company headquartered in San Jose, California, with a suite of business solutions covering creative tools, document management and creation, and digital marketing software. Since their founding in 1982, they had been a leader and continued that path in all their key product areas.

In sales cycles Dan often encountered Adobe, sometimes as a key competitor or a complementary solution. He knew their offering well and believed Adobe had the best all-round offering in the market for customer experience technology.

At the time, Adobe's hiring efforts had been focussed on well-established salespeople, rather than up and comers. When Dan first started his sales career, he would have struggled to get through the doors. As he now had a seven-year track record of relevant experience, Adobe quickly offered him the position, which came with a large pay increase. Offer accepted!

Although Dan understood Adobe's offering, he had a lot to learn. Their products are highly sophisticated compared to other vendors. Fortunately, Adobe has excellent training, which Dan took seriously and he studied hard to quickly build his knowledge. In addition, similar to what he did at Open Text, Dan developed his network in the organisation and learnt all that he could from his peers. Before long he was more than capable of leading sales cycles with confidence.

Dan's story from here has many resemblances to his time at Open Text; he grew from strength to strength and soon enough became one of the most respected Enterprise Account Executives in the EMEA (Europe, Middle East and Africa) sales region.

Now ten years into his sales career, Dan is a rare character who started his sales career in the right company at the right time, surrounded by Elite salespeople. His rapid development established firm foundations for him to become an Elite salesperson.

Dan Czasnicki's sales career wisdom

1. Understand what makes people successful in your role or the role you seek, develop that skillset and prove you can be that person.

2. Structure and hard work are key to success. Be organised.

3. Prove you are a person who people can trust by acting as a professional at all times.

COMMONALITIES OF THE ELITE

Haig, Mandy and Dan are three distinct people from unique backgrounds, yet all have become Elite salespeople. Did you identify commonalities between them? One thing is clear: their success was not an overnight process.

Take a moment to reflect:

- What is it that makes them different from the non-elite?
- What do they sell?
- Who do they sell to?

The vast majority of the sales profession sells low-value products to consumers or SMEs; it's a lot easier to do and, as a result, the financial rewards are significantly lower.

Elite salespeople almost only sell complex B2B solutions to mid-to-large enterprises and the value of the deals are in the tens of thousands, hundreds of thousands, or millions. The deal cycles are longer at 3, 6, 9, 12 or more months than an instant sale, or one that might take a few days. However, the commission checks are on a different scale.

To put it simply, the Elite treat their career as a profession and focus on continuous development in their career. Most people just see their job as 9 to 5, to pay the bills and give them enough money to have an OK lifestyle. For the Elite, this is inconceivable!

When you look at the commonalities of how the Elite built their careers, you'll uncover the *Pillars of an Elite Sales Career*. Interestingly, most Elite salespeople didn't even know they were building these pillars throughout their careers, they just did it. Imagine the difference it would have made if they had had this knowledge early in their careers. All 50 that I contacted, in their own words, wholeheartedly agreed that it would have saved them years.

Not only will you learn what these pillars are in this book, you will learn how to develop them and fast track your career. This takes commitment. First, you need to ask yourself some hard questions.

Why do you want this? What would it mean to you if you were an Elite salesperson? Money, success, recognition, supporting your loved ones, lifestyle, something else?

Be clear about what it is. Commitment has to have firm foundations or when the going gets tough, it is likely you will give up. Take your time, reflect, and have this point clear in your head. When you're clear on your 'why', it's time to get serious—are you prepared to do the following:

- Work harder than you've ever worked before, including early mornings, late finishes and intensive work?

- Constantly educate yourself and develop your skillset?

- Face failure after failure yet get back up again, with a smile on your face and more strength than before, to crush whatever lies in front of you?

- Humble yourself, learn from your mistakes and learn from those around you?

- Own your career and make hard decisions to move your life forward?

Yes?

Fantastic! To set expectations, for every pillar I will provide practical advice on how you can build this pillar into your own career. Just reading them will be worthwhile in its own right, but if you want to get the most from this, I highly recommend you slow down, write down your answers, and complete the tasks. You will see the difference.

Not convinced?

Towards the beginning of my sales career I read a book that changed my life: '*The Art of Closing the Sale*' by Brian Tracey. This book teaches you how to be a professional salesperson, and even though it was published in 1985, it's still highly relevant. At the end of every chapter, Brian leaves you with a series of questions of how to implement that knowledge in your own career.

I imagine 90% or more of people didn't do that, but I did. Two years in a row, I doubled my income.

Write it down.

Let's get started!

CHAPTER 3

HEART OF THE ACTION

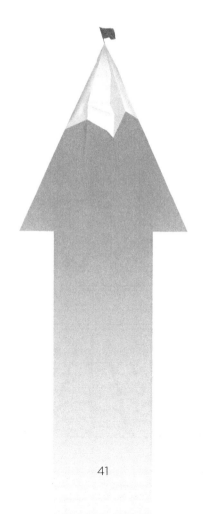

Never had the world seen such a mass migration of people in modern history in peaceful times than in 1849. People travelled far and wide, from Latin American countries, China, Europe, Australia, and every corner of North America. Half by sea and half by land, on the promise of a spectacle. The destination was California, and San Francisco in particular. The travellers became known as the 49ers.

This was the start of the largest gold rush the world has ever seen, which transformed America's economy and the lives of tens of thousands of its citizens.

One of the biggest winners of this period was a man named Samuel Brannan. He uncovered some interesting information when he discovered that James Marshall, a trusted foreman for a pioneer of the time, named John Sutter, had discovered gold on his land in the American river. Sutter rightfully feared that if news of gold got out, it would destroy his agricultural ambitions in the region, so he tried to silence Brannan. Brannan ignored this. He started a one-man rally shouting, 'Gold! Gold! Gold, from the American river', whilst holding a vial of gold. Brannan's main goal was to sell gold-prospecting equipment, which was the seed of his vast fortune. His largest financial gains came from property investments, fuelled by his gold equipment venture.[1]

It wasn't long until the *New York Herald* caught hold of the news, triggering this monumental event.[2] Excitement spread across the globe. People made more in six months than six years of their jobs back home. They literally made thousands of dollars per day. This stimulated the local economy, and its under-developed towns—with populations of only a few hundred—grew into thriving mining communities with many thousands of inhabitants.

Scholars believe the biggest winners from the gold rush were the merchants, such as Samuel Brannan, who served these wealthy newly founded towns. Even farmers selling onions made over $160,000 per year.[3] Then there were bigger winners, such as Levi Strauss, the founder of the famous denim brand, who saw an opportunity to provide durable clothing for miners and they flocked to him. His jeans would remain a favourite for generations to come.[4]

As easy as it was to find initially, the available gold soon vanished and mining innovation boomed. The evolution looked something like this:

1. Simple pans allowed miners to scour the river for gold.

2. Channels were then dug out next to the rivers to clear the riverbed, making it easier to get what lay below.

3. Construction of railroads and steamships increased, to carry the vast quantities of gold to places such as New York to convert it into currency and transport the hordes of people to and from the prospecting sites.

4. Water jets scarred the land, expose gold from beneath the surface.

5. Finally, more sophisticated mining machinery and tools were developed to mine gold in more difficult-to-reach places, in large quantities.

This brief period of history lasted only from 1848 to 1852. What a time to be alive! Innovations developed at this time no doubt created fresh opportunities further afield. Imagine being a sceptic at the time and watching this opportunity pass you by!

Most people, in fact, did watch from the sidelines. Despite hundreds of thousands of people being directly involved, the fast movers left little for others. Hindsight is a wonderful thing! That said, we can't overlook the fact that the industrial age was littered with dangers and thousands died or were seriously injured as a result of the gold rush.

Let's think about more recent technological innovations and the wealth they can generate. Are things much different today? Do people still sit on the sidelines as huge opportunities unfold in front of them?

Can you imagine a world without the technology to which we have become accustomed? For example, our computers, the internet, online shopping, smartphones, apps and countless other technological innovations. How could anyone have missed out on what these opportunities had to offer? In fact, many people have! These technological advances were always coming. It was just a matter of time. To truly understand this and to prepare for future events, it's important to look back through history to understand how our digital world was formed. Before I do so, I must warn you that the beginning part of the story is slow. To make this a more enjoyable experience both for you as reader, but also for me as author, let's summarise the key events and keep the focus on commercial success.

EARLY HISTORY OF THE DIGITAL AGE

Commercial success is a key factor in any real innovation taking off because it funds its development.

Calculators were the grandfather of computers. The calculator's most basic concept has been in development since 1623, and at the outset it was only available to pioneers or the wealthy. The Industrial Revolution of the 18th and 19th centuries was a major catalyst for the development of the calculator. Almost all repetitive tasks in factories were being mechanised to allow mass production. Advanced calculations were at the core of this and doing these longhand became a burden.

In 1820 a Frenchman, Charles Xavier Thomas de Colmar, built his Arithmometer to meet this challenge.[5] The device could perform addition, subtraction, multiplication and, with some serious thought, division. Despite the device being large enough to cover one's desk, it was a big success and sold for 90 years. Yet the price point was still very high, which meant only large businesses or the very wealthy could buy them. This sparked the development of business machines to meet similar challenges, such as the typewriter, which was first launched by E. Remington & Sons in 1873.[6]

One of the most notable success stories of the time comes from an American inventor, Herman Hollerith, whose innovation paved the way for the digitised computer. The United States Census Bureau employed Hollerith to help calculate the size of the booming U.S. population. His insights made him realise that the existing method for calculating the census was highly inefficient, so he developed ideas for how it could be radically improved.

Over the next ten years he refined his ideas until he had something he felt would resolve the challenge. A punch card would collect data from citizens and an automated machine would then read that to record it. In 1884 he filed a patent and had to wait five years until it was finally granted, so in 1889 Hollerith was ready to go to market.[7]

His first client asked him to produce the health records for the city of Baltimore in Maryland, New York City, and for the state of New Jersey. The result? The fastest ever completion of the data, by an inconceivable comparison. This opened the opportunity to use his machine to calculate the 1890 U.S. census, which was the enormous opportunity he had seen from the beginning. It generated approximately 100 million cards that clerks used keypunches to punch holes in the cards, entering age, state of residence, gender, and other information from the returns. The project finished months early and well below budget. Herman Hollerith had just set the new standard. This was the catalyst of his success. Word quickly got out and Hollerith's Tabulating machine was sold in Canada, Norway, Austria and Britain, among many other countries, laying the foundations for the incorporation of his 'Tabulating Machine Company'.[8]

Advancements in technology continued and several players arose, one of which was the American Arithmometer Company founded by William Seward Burroughs, Thomas Metcalfe, Richard M. Scruggs, and William R. Pye in 1886.[9] Burroughs invented an adding machine and obtained a patent, which was reviewed in 1894 in the *Bankers' Magazine* as follows:

'An ingenious adding machine, recently introduced in Providence banks, is said to be infallible in results, and to do the work of two or three active clerks. Enclosed in a frame with heavy plate-glass panels, through which the working of the mechanism can be seen, the machine occupies a space of 11 by 15 inches and is nine inches high. On an inclined keyboard are 81 keys, arrange in nine rows of nine keys each. The printing is done through an inked ribbon.'[10]

They dominated the market and, by 1908, had a market share of 90%. Banks were their first market where they quickly achieved scale, before branching out into almost every vertical, as well as international markets such as the U.K. By 1907 Burroughs had manufactured 50,000 of the machines and that year sold 13,300 at prices ranging from $300 to $500.

With inflation, the $300 to $500 price in 1907 would be the equivalent of $8,552 to $14,253 in 2019, making total revenues in that year worth around $114m–$190m today.

Imagine you were a salesperson at this point in history. Most likely you'd be selling suits, shoes, business services, shipping services or whatever else was commonplace then. You catch wind of this fast-growth, high-impact niche. Demand so hot that diaries become unmanageable and commission pay-outs are some of the highest around. Would you carry on selling whatever it is you are selling or would you jump into this exciting niche? The story here is the same as the gold rush; most sat on the sidelines. However, the industry was still emerging; let's give them that at least.

Several of the entrepreneurs of these early business machines companies combined their companies to form the Computing-Tabulating-Recording company (CTR) in 1911. Ten years later, CTR rebranded to form International Business Machines Corporation, or IBM. IBM became one of the most significant innovators of the digital age.[11]

THE RISE OF THE DIGITAL AGE

The World Wars served as a catalyst for IBM's many innovations and commercial successes. During wartime, technological advancements speed up, because a country's resources are all focussed on the same thing: winning or, at the very least, survival. The best minds of the countries coalesce for this purpose.

Several computing inventions came out of World War 2. German messages were encrypted in code using a machine known as the Enigma Machine, several of which can still be seen in museums today.[12] A team led by Alan Turing, a brilliant mathematician working at Bletchley Park in the U.K., used a machine they called the 'Bombe' to break the code, despite daily variations in encryption methodology.[13] By so doing, they saved thousands of lives and arguably shortened the War by several years.

At the same time, the U.S. military were developing the forerunners of modern computing to help them complete the complex calculations required to design the atom bomb. Ultimately, this led to the devastating detonation by the U.S. military of the bomb at both Hiroshima and Nagasaki in 1945, causing Japan to withdraw from the War.[14]

Fortunately for humanity, the German Z4, a machine said to be dozens of years ahead of its time, was stopped in its tracks by the German defeat by the Allied troops. It later went on to useful service and can now be seen in the Deutsches Museum, Munich.[15]

After the war, unlike the U.K. government, the U.S. made its designs available to innovators and entrepreneurs, which allowed the technology to be used to tackle many commercial, scientific and accounting challenges, across many industries. The race for market dominance had begun.

In 1953 IBM launched the IBM 650, which took the market by storm. 1,800 units were sold at approximately $200,000 a piece, almost solely to universities and large businesses. These were career-defining times for the salespeople of IBM! Despite heated competition, IBM captured the crown with a 60% to 70% market share.

Subsequently, IBM redefined the computer industry in 1964 by launching the IBM System/360 which was a single operating system, initially supporting six IBM hardware applications.[16] It became THE operating system. Fortunately so, because the reported $5bn investment IBM put into this would have crippled the company, had it failed. What this meant was that a single infrastructure could exist across organisations, permitting software development on a common code base, and thus the birth of the enterprise software market.

At the time, factories had to lock up a lot of cash in stock to operate, which is bad for cash flow. After the launch of the IBM System/360, companies developed MRP (Material Requirements Planning) software which allowed oversight of the entire stock process, meaning that clients could keep stock levels down by tracking customer demand. By 1970, there had been 700 installations.

One problem with the IBM software was that it was often bespoke. The time to develop, install and maintain it made it costly for organisations.[17]

To address this, in 1972 SAP launched their standardised MRP system, which allowed faster and cheaper deployments. Soon after, they gained an international client base, which proved their assumptions. However, managing data caused headaches for the adopters of MRP, which led to the formation of Oracle. They launched an SQL relational database management system to address the problem. It quickly became the standard.

Throughout the 1980s, MRP became Manufacturing Resource Planning[18], and it addressed many use cases in human resources (HR), accounting, logistics, and more. JD Edwards led the drive to bring MRP onto shop floors and company distribution centres, coining a new name, MRPII. All the major players secured installations globally, deal after deal. The enterprise software market was hot!

The 1990s saw these disparate systems come together under one term, ERP

(Enterprise Resource Planning), to describe the systems that underpin an entire enterprise's activity with a single, defined data structure.[19] A spree of mergers and acquisitions took place and SAP, Oracle, JD Edwards, and Baan became industry giants.[20] The people who led the charge were enterprise software sales-people. As a result, their pay rapidly outstripped that of their counterparts in many other sectors.

At the same time, rising adoption of personal computing was generating the next major advance in enterprise software adoption. Intel gained exclusive rights to the 4004 computer chip after developing a CPU (Central Process-ing Unit) for a Japanese calculator company, Busicom.[21] They paid $60,000 for the chip. This might seem like an impressive deal for Busicom, but it was in fact a much better deal for Intel, who immediately marketed the 4004 to computer manufacturers so that they could develop the next wave of com-puting devices.

Despite this innovation, the likes of IBM showed no interest. They solely focussed on profiting from the booming enterprise computing market, not want-ing to explore the potential of personal computing. It took a computer hobbyist movement to spark the evolution by using Intel's chips to develop a wide vari-ety of computing devices.

Visionaries Bill Gates and Paul Allen saw an opportunity to go further. The pair developed a suite of applications for businesses that included the spreadsheet, word processor and Power Point, spawning the Microsoft Corporation. Micro-soft's early astronomical success came about by partnering with IBM, who had realised that they lacked this suite of applications. By agreeing to install them on IBM machines out of the box, Microsoft instantly became the standard.[22]

However, personal computers were still not a thing because the price point meant they were still reserved for large organisations or the very wealthy. Steve Jobs and Steve Wozniak dared to envision a world where every person had a computer at home and could access the same technology as the very best enter-prises. They founded Apple to make this vision a reality. The Apple1 was the start of Apple, which they launched out of Jobs' garage; the founders sold their most prized possessions to start the company. For Jobs, this was his van and for Wozniak, his complex calculator, no doubt powered by an Intel chip.

Apple sparked the personal computing revolution. By 1997, 35% of people in the United States owned a personal computer compared with 15% in 1990, which changed it from a luxury to a necessity.[23] But it wasn't just the personal computing market that soared, the small business market did too. Not having seen the potential previously, IBM and HP entered the market late, allowing Apple to largely dominate it.

The rise of the personal and small business computing market directly correlated with the accelerated growth of Enterprise software, by 1999:

- JD Edwards had over 4,700 customers in over 100 countries.

- Oracle had 41,000 customers worldwide.

- Over 50% of the HR market used PeopleSoft.

- SAP was the world's largest enterprise software company, employing over 20,500 people in over 50 countries.

- 2,800 of Baan's enterprise systems had been implemented at approximately 4,800 sites around the world.[24]

Enterprise salespeople formed the backbone of all these companies' successes and still to do the present.

Selling a transformational enterprise software project takes more than just being an excellent talker and closer of deals, although, of course, it helps! A salesperson has to understand the client's business, how the technology will resolve their challenges and how it will align internal stakeholders, for example. The bigger the problem and the clients scale as a business, the larger the project, thus contract value. The rewards for closing a large six- or seven-figure contract include significant commission, internal recognition and more. As a result, software sales has emerged as one of the hottest sales professions.

The modern computing era was here to stay, and had transformed the world for good.

THE CONNECTION OF THE INTERNET

In 1969 the Advanced Research Projects Agency (ARPA) of America started to transfer information digitally between universities and research establishments. This approach rapidly sped up collaboration as they no longer had to rely on the postal system. They called this the internet.[25]

But it wasn't until 1989 when the British scientist Tim Berners-Lee and his team invented the World Wide Web (WWW) whilst working at CERN, the European Particles Physics Laboratory.[26] The original purpose was for scientists to share large documents with one another in an instant. But CERN saw the enormous potential and in 1993 put the World Wide Web into the public domain.

However, accessing the internet was still a painful task. A team based in the U.S. National Center for Supercomputing Applications addressed this challenge and developed the world's first mainstream internet browser. It was so effective they formed Netscape Communications Corp to take it to market and by 1994 it was available for public use.[27]

Netscape was an enormous success, growing exponentially, doubling the number of users and the number of websites every few months. Email became part of daily life and businesses increasingly adopted the internet for commercial purposes. Netscape's success attracted competitors, and Microsoft, Firefox and Google, among many others, entered the scene.

The growth of the internet directly correlated with the growth of personal computers, symbiotically fuelling each other. Entrepreneurs took advantage of this opportunity and started to market and sell their products and services online. Many achieved remarkable success, which attracted the attention of investors. As a consequence, the decade between 1990 and 2000 saw the dotcom boom.[28] Entrepreneurs pushed the boundaries in almost every conceivable way to release the potential of the internet, founding companies such as Amazon, Google, eBay and many more iconic brands during this frenzy. In parallel, enterprise software companies gradually adopted the internet, making it easier for users of their software to access their applications.

The excitement blinded people to the reality and company valuations became increasingly overhyped. Metrics such as web traffic, brand awareness and returning visitors became more important than bottom-line profit. Business failures piled up and by the year 2000 much of the investment had dried up. This caused the famous dotcom bubble to burst, and 50% of the dotcom businesses closed their doors. For example, Amazon, a survivor and champion of this period, saw its share price fall from $100s to between $7 and $8. Few businesses can handle a crash like that.[29]

Despite the dotcom boom and bust, innovation did not stop. A former executive of Oracle, Marc Benioff, conceived an idea whilst swimming with dolphins in Hawaii, on a career break.

Enterprise software provided many benefits, but it was a massive burden and commitment for organisations. For example, clients had to install servers on-site, customise the software and continually invest in expensive training. The process took months and the cost was high. Rarely did clients see ROI in their first year. What if enterprise software could be as easy as Amazon?

Benioff returned to San Francisco with an outline business plan. Rather than installing enterprise software on servers, he believed it would be far better for an organisation to access the software via a website. Just like Amazon. Set-up would be instant, and clients would achieve an ROI within months.

The CRM market (Customer Relationship Management) was red hot and, prior to the dotcom crash, businesses were investing heavily. It was a natural leap for Benioff to apply his concept to this market. To create the product, however, he needed a technical co-founder. In 1999, Benioff met with Parker Harris and together they co-founded Salesforce.com. They branded the term SaaS (Software-as-a-Service).[30] What followed was the most epic David versus Goliath battle in tech history, between Salesforce and Siebel Systems.

Siebel Systems were a formidable competitor, having been founded in 1993 and having created the enterprise software CRM category. By 2002 they had a market capitalisation of $30bn and a 45% market share. That said, their sheer size was exactly the problem that led to their demise. An average installation of 1,000 licences took serious commitment from their clients and, when a recession hit in the early 2000s, projects across enterprises were for the large part put on hold.

This was Salesforce's opportunity. Their SaaS model meant that it was just as easy to deploy 1 user or 1,000 (if Salesforce's servers could handle that volume at the time!). Individual departments of large enterprises and SMEs quickly turned to Salesforce. Salesforce grew a telesales team that blitzed the market, signing deal after deal, taking market share from Siebel Systems. Imagine the roar in that sales office! The sales team had endless career growth opportunities as Salesforce pumped the profits back into the business and sought outside investment to fuel its growth.

Siebel Systems were too big to change direction and failed to execute a counterattack. Sales remained flat, their market share declined and the valuation of the company dropped to a fraction of its once $30bn value. Salesforce had hit Siebel Systems so hard that there was no coming back.

Oracle saw this as an opportunity to enter the CRM market. They scooped up Siebel Systems for a small $5.8bn. Spectators sat in anticipation as Marc Benioff's former mentor, Larry Ellison, CEO of Oracle, went head-to-head with his old mentee. Yet Salesforce was too far ahead; even Oracle failed to reignite Siebel Systems' former glory. David had defeated Goliath.[31]

This incredible story inspired the world. Thousands of entrepreneurs launched SaaS businesses that repeated smaller versions of this story, giving birth to the SaaS model.

Alongside the launch of Salesforce, social media and online communities emerged. Early players such as MSN, Bebo, Classmates.com and Yahoo! 360°, just to name a few, opened the market. The first true commercial success, a key component for mass adoption, was when Mark Zuckerberg launched Facebook in 2004, with revenues driven by advertising.

Advertising sales had long been a key vertical for salespeople and the rise of the internet meant ad budgets started to move online. Search engines and online publishers dominated digital ad sales.

Based on legacy print models, in the early days online publishers would serve an ad on their website for advertisers with no real understanding of who saw it. The more advanced publishers used data collected by cookies to better target ads. Yet the data collected was limited.

The difference with Facebook is that they have first-party data. When a user signs up, they share a lot of personal data and the interactions they have whilst logged in reveals a lot about their interests, connections and the person they are. Facebook surfaces this data to advertisers to help them fine-tune the targeting of their ads. The result is incomparable conversion rates and metrics compared with other online publishers. Facebook had developed an advertising product that might rival the market.[32]

Despite Facebook being a software-led company compared to sales-led, such as Salesforce, they built a sales army. Quickly, major brands moved more and more of their ad budgets to Facebook and all the leading ad agencies built out social advertising teams. Social advertising mainly meant via Facebook. With the immense surge in user growth and client acquisition, Facebook's ad sales rocketed.

Figure 1: The rapid rise of Facebook's annual revenue from 2009 to 2019

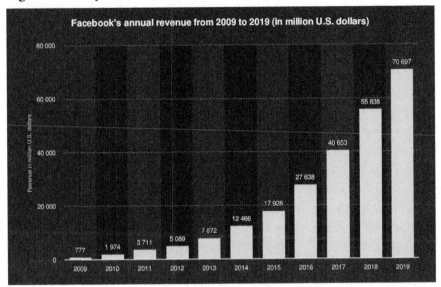

(Source: Statista 2020)[33]

Even though it's true that companies increase the size of their ad budgets over time, in terms relative to revenue growth, the reason so much revenue went to Facebook is because it was being taken away from traditional forms of advertising such as outdoors, print and television. Even so, there is no doubt that the salespeople on Facebook's ad sales team achieved remarkable success, including career-defining moments as they helped to launch this social media giant.

Other major social media commercial success stories include Twitter and LinkedIn. What is interesting about LinkedIn is that ad sales are just one of their revenue components and that the audience is of a professional nature, rather than consumer. They provide access to the largest online professional network in the world and sell subscriptions to salespeople and recruiters so they can better 'network' or, in better terms, sell to the other users. As with Facebook, the world had never seen a platform like this before, and 1,000s of LinkedIn salespeople fast-tracked their careers during this period at the company.

In 2007 Apple released the iPhone, which was a game changer.[34] The groundbreaking innovation of the smartphone wasn't just that it combined different technologies such as the camera, MP3 player, phone and internet access. It was the app store. The app store gave birth to a new way of interacting with brands and was one of the key triggers of the mobile revolution. Facebook, an early adopter, developed their app, which quickly became the most common way to access the site and the most commonly used app globally. Apps for just about anything appeared and mobile usage exploded, both domestic and commercial. By 2016, mobile accounted for most internet usage.

Broadbandandsearch.net has documented this historic moment in Figure 2.

Figure 2: Internet usage worldwide 2009 to 2016

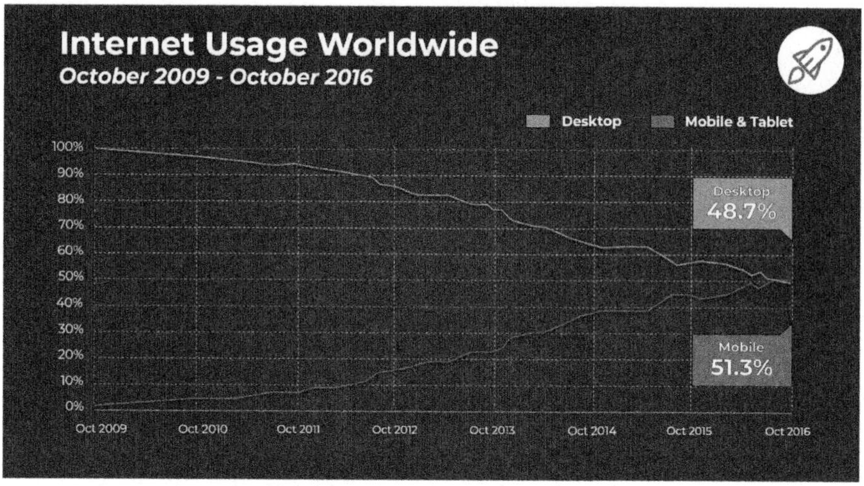

Internet Usage Worldwide
October 2009 - October 2016

Desktop — Mobile & Tablet

Desktop **48.7%**

Mobile **51.3%**

(Source: Broadband Search 2020)[35]

The digital era was here to stay and the role of the salesperson had evolved.

- Business machines drastically improved the way people completed manual tasks and the digital computer took this to the next level.

- Enterprise software transformed the way companies operate, increasing efficiencies and profits.

- The rise of the internet connected the world and sped up innovation at every turn. The mobile internet made it accessible for almost everyone around the clock.

Everything builds on top of each other, creating new disruptive opportunities. This constant drive keeps the pace of innovation moving at high speed.

Salespeople in technology are the change agent. When they successfully lead a client to proceed with their solution, the impact can be huge. Most of the time the benefits include reduced costs, increased sales or reduced risk, all of which give enterprises a competitive advantage.

DATA-DRIVEN WORLD

Data produced by digital activity underpins everything. Our internet footprints have skyrocketed during the digital era and this trend shows no sign of slowing down. Enterprises collect and store this data in huge quantities. The scale has become so significant that *The Economist* published a very interesting article in 2017 with the title 'The world's most valuable resource is no longer oil, but data'.[36]

Undoubtedly, the most valuable companies in the world as of this writing in 2020 are data driven. Think of Apple, Microsoft, Amazon, Google and Facebook, to name a selection.

This data-driven world has created new opportunities. Technologies such as Machine Learning, AI and NLP (Natural Language Processing) are enabling existing SaaS players to grow their platforms. In addition, new entrants to the market continually threaten to disrupt the incumbents. Innovation never ends and disruption is the nature of the tech industry, so it's in disruption where you will find Elite salespeople. Can you imagine being on the sales team for the IBM 360, or at Siebel Systems or Salesforce during their respective meteoric rises? Think of the prospects lining up to learn about your product, the competitors of no consideration, and commercial success like you'd never experienced!

This is a key pillar beneath Elite salespeople's career success. They place themselves in the heart of the action, the gold rush of their time. If you are too early to a market, your prospects won't move fast enough. Too late, and the competition will be too fierce to permit success. Timing is essential. To date, often big, recent technological innovation has started in the U.S., and when American firms look to expand into Europe, there's a large pool of sales talent hungry to lead the next wave of innovation.

Joachim Haas

Joachim Haas, from Germany, has built a career in launching American tech businesses in Europe and restructuring the ones that are struggling to achieve scale.

However, Jo, as he prefers to be known, has a very unlikely family history. He comes from a dynasty of priests and this is the path his mother would have loved him to pursue. This was not Jo's calling, however. Having always loved to talk and connect with people, Jo's career had to further this passion. Which is even more unlikely, since Germans were renowned for being incredibly reserved at that time, and quite different from Jo's eccentric nature.

After graduating from university, he joined a company called Pilot. They had founded the business intelligence market, which grew to become one of the most significant software verticals. Despite knowing very little about tech, the sales leader of the organisation saw something in Jo. He believed Jo had it in him to be exceptional and gave him a chance. This man became one of Jo's most influential mentors.

Within the first year, Jo achieved phenomenal success and made it to the Presidents Club, which is an incentive some companies offer to their top sales-people and is usually an all-expenses paid trip to a luxury resort for the weekend, or something similar. By year two in 1990, he was already earning six figures. Not only were Pilot impressed by Jo's growing skillset, but his clients were too. The CEO at one of them was so amazed that anyone could sell a product as poorly suited to their needs as what they had purchased, that he was eager to hire a salesperson that could pull off such a feat; he offered Jo a leadership posi-tion. The CEO was clearly a salesperson too! Subsequently, tasked with building up the partnership sales channel, in only a brief period Jo built it into a €10m annual business unit.

The rapid innovation in the tech industry meant that enterprise software was constantly upgraded, causing a big headache for the IT departments that had to manage the entire process. Managesoft was founded in Boston in 1990 to tackle this problem and achieved huge global success, with offices across the globe.

Unfortunately, the European operations hadn't started as planned. Five sales-people had just about secured five clients in five years... yes, you read that right! Jo's impressive record made it easy for Managesoft to hire him to restructure. Outraged at the team, Jo fired all five salespeople and decided that, before hir-ing anyone else, he had to prove the model himself.

In three years, Jo secured 55 new clients, lost only one deal and hired no other salespeople. Three sales engineers supported him in handling the tech-nical and administrative parts of the deals, and between them could manage an incredible workload. In most sales organisations one sales engineer covers between three and five salespeople, but Jo had turned the model on its head and successfully established Managesoft in Europe.

The pace of the market meant organisations were ready to spend and Jo and his team convinced them that Managesoft was the right option. A main contributor to his success was that he just focussed on doing what he loved, speaking with people. Jo always aims to connect with people's hearts and minds. His team supported him in doing exactly that and they won together.

After this, Jo was ready for his next challenge. His parting gift to the chief information officer (CIO) were industry insights that led to product enhancements and changes to pricing. Shortly after, in April 2010, Flexera, the global giant in this space, acquired Managesoft.[37]

During this time Jo learnt something about himself. As businesses grow, new layers of management come in and, as a leader, you become increasingly separated from your team. Jo leads from the front and is energised when he is side by side with his salespeople. His success pulled him away from what he loves doing. In the years that followed, Jo focussed on his sweet spot, the initial phases of launch. Similar success stories followed.

Joachim Haas's sales career wisdom
---

1. Go deep, immerse yourself and learn everything you can about your space.

2. Challenge yourself, don't be afraid to fail and, when you do, make sure you learn fast and get back up on your feet.

3. Most importantly, find a mentor. You'll need the guidance to progress.

Jo's passion is to sell and he has built a very successful career on that basis.

From the beginning of his career Jo was in tech. Not all Elite salespeople start their careers in the same manner.

Ben Tunstall

Some of us decide higher education is not essential for success, despite what society tells us. Ben Tunstall, at 18, made that bold decision and pursued a career in sales straight after school. Given his character, it did not surprise his friends and family.

Ben was open to any opportunity that would take him as long as they had mentors to mould him. His first move was selling mobile phone contracts at a mobile reseller to small businesses. Occasionally he would land a big fish, although whether that was by luck or skill, he was unsure.

Driving down the motorway passing vehicle after vehicle, for most of us, triggers no emotion or thought. For Ben Tunstall, these were leads. He would examine the company brands of commercial vehicles and when he identified one he hadn't seen before, he would pull out his dictaphone and record the company name. On arriving back home, he would listen back to the recording and write out the names. This helped fuel his target list the next morning, on top of the list of companies he would target in an old, yet famous, English business directory, the Yellow Pages.

On Monday mornings Ben's calves got strong. His company made him and his colleagues stand until they had made a certain number of calls and booked a certain number of meetings. Sounds harsh, but it engrained sales discipline in him, which has helped to shape his career. At least he didn't have to tape the phone to his hand. As unlikely as this sounds, it did used to happen in some extreme sales offices. The good old days!

After a successful start, he decided he could be a lot more successful if he worked for the provider themselves, so he moved directly to Three Mobile, where his career progression accelerated. So well in fact, that at 20 Ben was promoted to team leader, after an opportunist decision to put his name forward. He oversaw a team of people at least ten years his senior.

Good things don't last forever. Ben had entered the mobile contracts sector at a great time, there were a lot of new accounts to go after and competition was only starting to heat up. Several years in, he felt the market had become saturated and mobile phone contracts a commodity. For a salesperson, this isn't a great place to be; you soon become an order taker. This motivated Ben to look for his next opportunity.

During this path, and for the first time in his life, Ben met a truly inspiring leader. Someone who was part of the Elite, someone who could help guide him to becoming the best that he could be. Let's call this man George.

George was the sales leader of a mobile security software company, Good Technology, later acquired by Blackberry. Because of the surge in mobile phone adoption in businesses, mobile security was high on the agenda for enterprises that had sensitive data to protect. Good Technology's growth exploded. To capitalise on the opportunity, they sought top salespeople.

After interviewing Ben, George saw huge potential in him. He was impressed by what he had achieved at such a young age in terms of sales and his knowledge of mobile. George made Ben an offer he couldn't refuse. It wasn't just the money; it was the opportunity to learn and become part of an A-player team. Top salespeople on the team were earning more than £500,000 a year.

During this process, Ben had secured a promotion with Three, for which he'd worked exceptionally hard. As exciting as that was, it wasn't nearly as exciting as the opportunity with Good Technology. Ben made the move.

As you can probably imagine, it sucked him into what felt like a whirlwind. Eager to make a name for himself, he lived outside of his comfort zone and aimed to surpass expectations at every turn. For a junior Account Executive, they gave him a fairly large target, near enough $1m. In addition to his day job, Ben was asked to build 'the channel', which of course he agreed to, with a smile on his face. Ben did not understand what 'the channel' meant and had no idea how to build one.

The channel refers to establishing partnerships with other businesses in your space that will either resell or refer you business. A salesperson's role in the channel is to recruit new partners and train them to be effective in reselling your offering, referring you business, or both. Leads will either be passed to other salespeople on the team or you'll help the partner secure them yourself. It's common to find that companies with a more established channel strategy split the team in two, recruiting partners and managing them.

Alongside Ben's day job of trying to secure businesses with under 2,000 employees in the U.K. (a huge patch) as clients, he built a successful channel. However, the referral opportunities generated were not his alone and he was incredibly disappointed to learn that he would not be compensated for this additional work. The worst thing about it was the distraction meant he could not overachieve his target; he only scraped his target that year. With Good Technology growing at such a rapid pace, he felt he wasn't getting the mentorship he'd signed up for, which for him was a key part of the deal.

Now in his early twenties, Ben had learnt some key lessons and had some cash behind him. He had had a strong start to his sales career, so took a short career break with some friends to go skiing for six months. This time out really gave him the opportunity to relax, refocus and get ready for the next rollercoaster. At this stage it was clear to Ben how he would develop his career. He'd met some of the best in the industry, they'd welcomed him onboard and he'd had a solid start. To become one of these people, he needed an environment where he could grow. That environment took him by surprise.

The technology market in London was booming. It wasn't just the tech companies that were enjoying this growth, but also recruitment companies. CD Recruitment, a long-established player in recruiting tech salespeople, quickly offered Ben a position to place the A-players he sought to emulate into top tech companies. As these types of people will earn well into six figures, they command a high base, anywhere from £60,000–£120,000 and double OTE (On Target Earnings). Recruitment companies are paid a percentage of the person's base as a commission, which can be anywhere from 10% to 20% and they would then pay their recruiters a percentage of that percentage. It paid pretty well to place A-players, so well that top recruiters at CD earnt six figures annually.

Ben ramped up fast, given his experience. Day by day he was inspired by the success these A-players in tech sales had achieved. It furthered his ambition to be like them.

The commonalities in these people became clear. It wasn't long before Ben's confidence reached a level where he felt ready to be one of them. That said, he was in no rush to move; he was earning good money. Yet he was open for the right opportunity.

Recruitment experience was in demand for a hyper-growth company by the name of LinkedIn. They approached Ben with a position to account manage large recruitment companies that had signed up to LinkedIn's premium offering, an offering Ben used every day himself. Intrigued by the opportunity, he arranged a call. Soon into that call he was sold on LinkedIn. This is exactly the company that he wanted to work for.

Yet Ben declined the opportunity. From his experience, the best salespeople are in new business. He asked LinkedIn to get back in touch when they had a new business role.

Six months later the recruiter got back in touch with a new business position, and immediately Ben put himself forward; never had he felt so prepared for an opportunity. LinkedIn changed the trajectory of his career; the constant challenge and need to learn fuelled him. He hit the ground running, deal after deal, quota after quota, crushed. His earnings reached a level he had only dreamed of a few years ago. Ben had finally become an A-player.

After a while, the rapid pace of his development slowed. Sure, he was making more than £300,000 a year and loved what he did, but without the rapid pace of development in himself, Ben got itchy feet. Despite the success he had now achieved, he knew that he was only scratching the surface. After three years at LinkedIn, he took his time to identify the next opportunity, but this time it was on his terms. He was interviewing companies rather than them interviewing him.

Cloud computing to many is the norm, so why deploy software differently? The reality is that, even back in 2018, cloud computing only accounted for 30% of software deployed. Many large companies such as banks, airlines, government organisations, oil companies and more operated on legacy software applications in a digital-first world. The growing problem these companies had was being able to access data within their legacy platforms and integrate it into cloud applications to deliver on use cases across the organisation. For most organisations, this data resided in their data warehouse.

Data warehouses, one of the largest software categories, were mostly deployed on-premise, until Snowflake came along. They had brought to market the first true enterprise-grade SaaS data warehouse and were blitzing the market. Now it was time to expand into EMEA, with a London-based headquarters.

When Ben learnt about the opportunity, he saw this as a sure way to step outside of his comfort zone and grow. At LinkedIn he learnt a lot about how data powered their products and the benefits of cloud computing. Yet he hadn't learnt how to guide a company through a digital transformation project and that was the challenge that excited him.

Ben thought he'd met the Elite by now, but when he interviewed at Snowflake the Elite of the Elite greeted him. He was convinced Snowflake would be the place to take his career to the next level and they were convinced Ben was ready to take that step. With much to learn, but a lot to gain, Ben is back in his comfort zone of being uncomfortable, in the heart of the action.

——————————————— **Ben Tunstall's sales career wisdom** ———————————————

1. Be prepared to learn.

2. Throw yourself in at the deep end.

3. Put in the graft and, above all, commit yourself.

FOCUS ON THE HEART OF THE ACTION

Just as most salespeople end up in the profession, they equally end up in a given market. Most are first focussed on working for an excellent company that pays well, where they can progress their careers. Sometimes these companies are in the heart of the action, but not always, and that is the risk. The pace of both the market and the organisation have an enormous influence on the pace at which you build your career.

In sales it's a lot easier to be successful in a vertical where many enterprises have projects to resolve problems that your solution addresses. It means that they are ready to invest. The bigger the problem, the bigger the investment and the larger the financial rewards for the salesperson.

Most do not consider these economic opportunities and, as a result, do not achieve their potential. Be someone that does and you'll see the difference in your sales results. If you are just starting this journey or perhaps you are already well into it, but your goal is to ramp up your success, identify where the heart of the action is.

Here is how:

1. Conduct a research project on a fast-growth and substantial market and understand what the most promising categories within it are.

2. Decide which categories excite you most and explore those further. Is that space innovating? Are the products widely adopted (being too early is tough!)? Is there still room for huge growth (growth = money)?

3. Within the category that gets you most excited, with the most promise, identify the leading companies and the rising stars.

Not sure where to start? It's as straightforward as a Google search. You will uncover many interesting reports and publications written on the subject that will help answer your questions.

One such research company you are likely to encounter is Gartner, an IT consultancy firm. In 2008 they first published the 'Magic Quadrant', a series of market research reports that ranks vendors in each software category. To make their assessment, Gartner uses proprietary qualitative data analysis methodology.[38]

Figure 3: Gartner Magic Quadrant

As you can imagine, there are many of these quadrants, given the vast number of software categories.

Such a project is no minor task, yet it will set you up for success and give you a mature perspective on the market. That perspective will not only prime you for success, but earn you respect amongst your leaders and clients.

A word of warning. You will most likely encounter companies that are launching new innovations to market, often early stage start-ups. If this attracts you, make sure they have proven use cases and that the larger organisations are adopting the technology. If you enter these promising tech markets too early, it can slow down your success; it's better to join them as the party is kicking off. Think about going to a bar. Who wants to be the first there? Equally, who wants to be the last and risk missing the party? Timing is important.

For a deeper understanding on the topic, I highly recommend that you read Geoffrey Moore's best-selling book, *Crossing the Chasm*.[39] Moore shares his findings on the 'Technology Adoption Lifecycle' and what happens at each stage. As a salesperson, you want to be in either the early or late majority stage of the lifecycle. Deals will be bigger, sales cycles shorter and the volume of leads higher. As a result, you will maximise your sales and thus your earnings.

Once you have homed in on the space that excites you the most, the one with the most promise, compare that to the company and industry you are in today and ask yourself the hard questions.

- Are you truly in the right place to guarantee your success?

- What will your life look like one, three and five years from now if you focus on this hot space that you've identified?

- What's stopping you from making that move?

- If you already are in that hot space for one of the top companies, fantastic! Focus on where you are and be even more confident of your success. If not, make a transition plan.

Research the top companies, understand the positions available and figure out how you might market yourself to them. You might have to gain further experience or start at a more junior position. Or perhaps you are ready to just go for it.

Recruiters are often a superb way in. But if you already know which companies you want to apply for, you will increase your chances by applying directly and showing genuine interest in that company. Whatever you do, don't just send a C.V. as your leading approach; that's what everyone else does. A better approach is to contact the senior sales leaders of these organisations directly, who you would be likely to report to.

To identify them, use LinkedIn or conduct a Google search. Once you have identified target individuals, craft a personalised message that explains why you want to work for that company in that industry, stating your (genuine) admiration for the person and why you are the right fit to work for them. If you can find a phone number for the person, call them directly to deliver the message. If not, directly message them on LinkedIn or via email. Be creative in how you deliver the message to make yourself stand out. Show them you are a salesperson. Failing this, pursue another approach and don't give up. This position will give you the opportunity to not only fast track your career, but arguably every aspect of your life.

Another way in could be to leverage employee referral schemes. Fast-growth organisations often reward commission to those employees who introduce new team members. So why not take advantage of this? Identify senior salespeople in the organisation and approach them. Focus on those that seem successful because they're likely to have a better reputation in that company. This means they will be a stronger ally to help you secure the role.

Again, show admiration for what they've achieved and why you are passionate about joining their organisation. Ask for a chat to pick their brains on how you can get a position at the company. Not very many people will do this, so your message will stand out and if you gain credibility with this person, it's likely they'll help you. Remember, they get paid if you get the job and pass probation.

One last idea. Employees of leading companies attend conferences and, more often than not, the leaders of these companies will be there. Identify which events the sales leaders you'd like to meet attend and go there intending to introduce yourself in person. Can you imagine how impressed they will be with that level of dedication? OK, it might be a challenge to find them, but what have you got to lose? The point is, be creative and don't give up. Do what it takes to place yourself in the heart of the action.

CHAPTER 4

INDUSTRY EXPERT

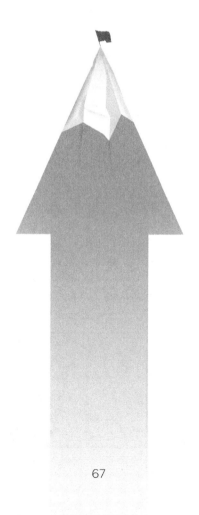

L ife continually throws curve balls at us. At the worst of times, it takes more than a simple Google search to answer our problems; sometimes we require an expert. For example, perhaps our car has broken down. Most people would head straight to a mechanic to have the problem assessed and fixed to get their vehicle back on the road. Or maybe we have become unwell. When the problem is sufficiently bad, we have no choice but to face the long waiting times of our respective health services. A doctor will diagnose the issue and recommend an appropriate course of action to get you back on your feet. But sometimes the issue is severe and goes beyond a doctor's general knowledge. In which case, they recommend a specialist.

The human body is hugely complex. The thought of one person having all the answers, no matter the issue, is impossible. Therefore, we have specialists, whether that be cardiologist, dermatologist, neurologist, paediatrician, and the list continues. This specialist will probably do further analysis and, upon making discoveries about the issue, will recommend a course of treatment until their patient is back to good health, in the best of cases.

Professions such as law or accountancy are not much different, relying as they do on expertise and in-depth knowledge of a subject. The journey to becoming a specialist takes time—a lot of time. Fortunately for them, the knowledge they possess comes with a premium price tag. In a B2B sales environment, it's really not that much different.

THE VALUE OF INDUSTRY KNOWLEDGE

Let's take the example of a CMO (Chief Marketing Officer), that we will call Adam. He works for a fast-growth travel brand that specialises in selling discounted luxury holidays, called Bargain Retreats. Their rapid growth has caused growing pains. These plague them with manual processes in their digital marketing department that makes scaling campaigns slow and expensive. More nimble competitors have out-competed them on campaigns, so much that some campaigns have reported a negative ROI. To ensure continued success, they must become more agile.

After evaluating their processes, Adam and his team conclude that they require a marketing automation platform. It will allow them to scale faster and be more agile. He secures board approval. This leads the marketing, loyalty, IT, web and data and business intelligence teams to work together to create an RFP (Request For Proposal). Approximately five serious vendors meet their criteria, all of which receive the RFP.

One automatically withdraws, leaving four in the race.

One vendor submits the RFP within a week. Two request an initial meeting to better scope the RFP, and one goes silent.

The first vendor is Adapt CX, the No. 1 vendor in the Gartner Magic Quadrant. The account executive leading the RFP is a diligent man named Harry, who has been in tech for over ten years working with leading brands. The first meeting is in fact a call, during which it is clear that Harry has taken the time to understand the RFP and carefully takes his time to examine the deeper issues underlying Adam's challenges. The outcome is a meeting in which Harry can present exactly how Adapt CX will help resolve Bargain Retreats' challenges and so the RFP is sent later that week.

Next up is Targetmate, which is a close second in the Gartner magic quadrant. Danielle is the account executive and she takes a similar approach to Harry. She, however, gets Adam to think of the problem differently. He is so focussed on the task at hand that he hasn't evaluated the new marketing campaigns Bargain Retreats will be able to launch with a marketing automation platform. Danielle shares relevant examples and inspires Adam.

Harry and Danielle both have meetings locked in to present their solutions and submit the RFP.

Jenny from Datawizz, who had submitted the RFP in record time, arranges a call to talk through it with Adam. He needs a little more time, as it was quite a comprehensive answer, but invites Jenny to come and present their offering, and she accepts.

On the big day, the three vendors who responded are booked in back to back to present to the Bargain Retreats marketing and tech teams. The fourth vendor messages that morning, apologising for the slow reply. It is late in the process, so Adam says he will get back to them if the three presenting aren't the right fit. In plain English, they are out of the race.

Up first is Danielle from Targetmate, joined by her solutions engineer who handles the more technical side of discussions. Danielle begins by reframing the conversation. She gets Adam and his team to look at the bigger picture. The big pay-off is not just being more effective and agile on existing campaigns, it's launching new ones that their competitors will struggle to do. To follow, Danielle and her solutions engineer deliver an eye-opening demonstration.

Next Jenny from Datawizz, again joined by her solutions engineer. She gets straight into it and delivers Datawizz's proposition flawlessly, which is a good fit for Bargain Retreats. She teases them with a new AI feature that helps to predict who is most likely to buy. If they can move quickly, she offers them the opportunity to join the Beta programme.

To end the day, the much-expected Harry and the Adapt CX team step in. He receives a warm welcome, as Harry has worked with James, the head of loyalty before. Adapt CX are no strangers to tough competition, so they come prepared and well educated on how best to present their solution to resolve Bargain Retreats' problems.

Bargain Retreats are blown away; they realise why Adapt CX is rated so highly. Harry and his team demonstrate Adapt CX's highly robust platform and how it can deliver on almost all use cases. With an impressive list of clients, they share some relevant case studies.

The following day, Bargain Retreats analyse which vendor is the best fit. Despite how well Jenny from Datawizz presented and diligently answered their questions, they decide Datawizz isn't the best fit. Datawizz are out of the race.

The decision is now Targetmate or Adapt CX and there is not much in it. Bargain Retreats believe both vendors can help them achieve their goals. Adam shares the news and requests a final proposal from each.

Targetmate comes in at a slight price premium. Yet Danielle did something that gives Targetmate the edge. She helped Bargain Retreats to think bigger and demonstrated how they could achieve more with Targetmate's platform today and tomorrow. It gives them the edge and Targetmate is selected as the preferred vendor.

Adapt CX is not out of the race yet, so a tough negotiation begins. Both vendors are keen to secure a brand in the spotlight such as Bargain Retreats and a deal worth more than £300,000 that will take a nice chunk off their targets.

Harry knows he is on the back foot and if he is to lose, decides to make it painful for Targetmate. He drops the price by 30% and offers guaranteed access to some new, highly relevant features. He positions the reserve budget to be spent on ads. It causes a divide in the Bargain Retreats team.

Danielle has one last opportunity to close the deal, so she reinforces the value of her offer. Do you want to continue to compete on the same playing field as your competitors or do you up the game? Gritting her teeth, she fights internally for a 12% discount, which is time bound. Despite the discount, Targetmate is still more expensive.

Crunch time. Who would you choose if you were Adam? This isn't a simple decision; both are exceptional vendors and are represented by Elite salespeople.

Adapt CX is without doubt a safe choice. But Targetmate's unique positioning gives them the edge, despite the price premium.

Targetmate wins!

When you represent industry leaders, expect your competition to be of a similar calibre, which means that underestimating them can be fatal. Clients seek people who can educate them, add value and help them with their problems. This is a must. Sometimes as sellers we overestimate the buyer. It's our responsibility to not only know our product inside out, but to know our industry in-depth and have our own perspective. It's our responsibility to lead the client. This is what it means to be an expert. Danielle did that better than Harry and therefore she won the deal. Her leadership gave Bargain Retreats the confidence to go with Targetmate.*

So, what is the path to becoming an industry expert? To begin, I can assure you that it doesn't happen overnight. Experts are well tenured. Their stories involve many career building blocks.

Steve Mason

Steve Mason had, from a young age, exposure to the sales industry, as he was

---

* Disclaimer: This is a fictional story with fictional characters and brands. That said, there are many elements of truth in this story derived from my own and others' experiences.

a keen drummer and at school had set up a drum school for local kids. Alongside that, he had a paper round and, as he got a little older, would work part-time as an estate agent in his parents' business. Little did he know that these odd jobs would shape his career.

During university, Steve and his peers were encouraged to seek internships, so Steve secured his with Hewlett Packard (HP), an American computer manufacturer with a strong European presence, headquartered in London.

After graduating, he had a clear idea of what he wanted to do with his career, which was to go into IT sales. During his internship, he had worked with one of HP's partners, who were keen to offer him a junior sales position selling HP equipment to SMEs. Steve jumped at the opportunity, but soon found himself in at the deep end! It was no surprise to him it would be a challenge to learn how to be a professional salesperson. What was a surprise was the complexity of the solutions he'd be selling.

To learn the products, many would read manuals, take courses etc, but Steve took a novel route. He networked with the techies and learnt hands-on how to take apart and assemble a server, amongst other hardware. If you'd have walked past, you'd have assumed Steve was a techie too: surrounded by computer parts, connecting pieces of hardware together, wiring the kit, with a look of pure concentration on his face. That said, in his earlier attempts you'd probably think that this man was out of his mind, that he might injure himself or others with the way he was approaching the task! Yet he persevered and eventually got there.

Steve was thankful that he did. This new level of knowledge allowed him to rapidly gain credibility with technical buyers, which was most of them. As a result, he won business and before he knew it, he'd crushed his sales targets, outpacing his peers.

After some time had passed, he felt that his career progression was lacking. The organisation only had about 100 employees and was run by two brothers who rarely sold to large enterprises, which Steve knew was where the big money was.

Around this time, a LinkedIn recruiter approached Steve with an interesting opportunity to join a fast-growth IT reseller. The difference with this company was that they sold several brands, including HP, and provided a range of IT services. Their focus was on large enterprise clients and they had many contracts worth seven figures or more. Without doubt, this appeared to be the opportunity that Steve was seeking to take his career to the next level. He applied and secured the role.

Steve learnt one of his most valuable skills at this point in his career. When you work on large, complex deals, it requires close collaboration with clients. Building initial trust is the first part, but developing the relationship and becoming a trusted advisor is when the true success happens. Steve's role was in sales, but he became so closely involved with his client's business that they saw him as part of their team. Within the first couple of years, he had secured several multi-million pound accounts and joined the Elite in sales. At that time, the company was experiencing phenomenal growth, so much so that it grabbed the attention of BT, who acquired them for a tidy sum. It was this success that prompted Steve to leave his job, as the thought of working for an enormous company like BT made him shiver.

With the rapid rise of the internet and cloud computing, the demand for data centres skyrocketed. It was in this wave that Steve found his next opportunity. A small data centre consulting firm in Nottingham saw this market opportunity. To capture a noteworthy market share, they required a sales leader who knew how to close business. Steve applied for the role. Quickly this company decided that Steve was the man to take them forward and made him an offer, which he accepted. The opportunity excited him! Although that excitement soon dwindled...

The market opportunity was there and companies were spending millions on data centres, but Steve felt this consulting firm wasn't the right company to be a significant player in this race. Their culture was that of a small organisation and they didn't share his hunger to grow. In addition, the commute from London to Nottingham every day was a headache!

Many would have hopped jobs to a better-suited organisation to continue their growth trajectory, but Steve paused and questioned what he was doing with his life. In reality, he wasn't that passionate about IT services. He enjoyed it and was good at it, but didn't truly care. Instead, he wanted to make a small difference to the world. After some soul-searching, he found his passion in the health and life sciences sector. He felt that supporting these organisations to grow would have a positive impact on the world. Many IT-related companies in the sector were hiring. The one that stood out the most to Steve was IMS Health. Their offering is a suite of tools for drug manufacturers and research labs. These tools allow for better analysis of data and they speed up the development process of drugs. Clients achieved remarkable results. This inspired him and he became determined to secure the role, intensively researching the company and the wider industry to prepare for the opportunity. Step by step in the recruitment process, he impressed his potential employer. They offered him a role and four weeks later he started.

As with Steve's first sales role in which he sold IT hardware, he was well and truly in at the deep end, because this was a whole new world for him. To get up to speed, he took a humble approach. He sought several mentors, not just within IMS but at his clients too. Imagine a salesperson who, instead of just trying to sell to you, asks if you can help them learn the industry so they can better serve you! Impressed by his humility, they helped him, and soon enough he learnt the language, how to navigate these complex organisations, and what was important for them. Again, he reached the status of a trusted advisor amongst his clients.

These deep insights gave Steve an edge and success quickly followed. He enjoyed several years with IMS Health and became deeply immersed in the health and life sciences industry. Deep experience in high-value industries such as this increases your value as a salesperson. Few can call themselves experts.

Steve came to the attention of Salesforce, the pioneers of cloud computing. They had gained immense success in almost every industry except health and life sciences. It was a weak point for them, which they focussed on resolving by creating industry-specific teams. Salesforce Marketing Cloud at the time was achieving rapid growth and the leadership team saw this as a strategic way to enter the health and life sciences market, yet they lacked someone with the relevant tech and industry experience. Their recruiters found Steve's profile and, impressed by his experience, approached him.

Although Steve was in no rush to leave IMS, when a company like Salesforce knocks on your door, it's at least worth a chat. When he learnt about Salesforce's innovative and progressive culture, it connected with his values. They use business as a driving force to make the world a better place. Here he could make a larger impact than at IMS. Salesforce was not only where Steve's core values would align, but he would be surrounded by the best in the industry. The cherry on top was the large increase in pay. He made the move.

Penetrating new accounts with a solution that the industry was just about ready for was a challenge. He learnt an incredible amount and had fantastic sales leaders to help guide him. Gradually he broke into accounts and worked his network to accelerate his success. That said, it wasn't quite the rockstar entrance he had become accustomed to. After some time, Steve felt that the culture in Salesforce had changed. With rapid growth and an acquisition spree, it became a lot more about the sales numbers than the company's mission. This misaligned with Steve's reason for joining them and he started to look for another role.

In companies that experience rapid growth (or other restructure), especially large corporates, it is not uncommon for internal dynamics to change. Steve's account is not a negative statement on Salesforce, simply his personal experience.

One of Steve's old sales leaders joined a seed investment-backed AI-based start-up in the manufacturing space to lead the growth. Steve hadn't done the start-up thing before at a tech company and was excited by the opportunity, so he joined too. Shortly after that, the sales leader he admired left! Slightly alarmed but unfazed, he pressed on and secured their initial clients, a huge milestone for any tech start-up. Despite these early wins, he felt that he wasn't set up for success. The pace of growth was not on a par with what he had become accustomed to at the likes of HP partners, IMS Health and Salesforce, so this hadn't been the best move for him. Yet with personal financial commitments, Steve persevered.

At Heathrow Terminal 5 Steve was awaiting a flight to see a major prospect. While there, he stumbled across an old colleague from IMS who was now working at Veeva as a sales leader, whom we'll call Andrew. Never had Andrew seen Steve in a negative place—he'd always remembered Steve as a positive person who brings energy to the room. As Andrew heard more about Steve's career challenges, he shared a little about Veeva and the rocket ship that they were on. Intrigued, Steve agreed to meet him again for a chat.

Veeva made sense to him. Their focus is purely on health and life sciences and the CRM technology they sell relates well to Steve's experience. What excited Steve beyond the natural synergy was that Veeva was on a rapid growth track, they were an industry leader, and had a lot more growth ahead of them. By far, this would be the best move of Steve's career to date.

At the end of my interview with Steve he was in his first year at Veeva. He has zero regrets in moving there, only excitement for what is coming. There are a few things he wishes he'd known sooner in his career, that he recommends others should do when aiming to build their Elite sales career.

Steve Mason's sales career wisdom

---

1. Find your passion as soon as possible. When you align your core values, it allows you to tap into your full potential and trigger a higher sales performance.

2. Once you find this thing go deep, you need to become an expert. Once you are an expert it will allow you to become a trusted advisor which is a cut above the rest.

3. With both things aligned, you then need people to buy into you and your vision. Develop your public speaking and presentation skills.

A last nugget of wisdom from Steve; along his path he has had some hard knocks, has been pulled off key accounts, made the wrong job move, lost inspiration, and so on. When this happens, it seems like the world is crushing in on you. Everything you've worked so hard for, everything you've sacrificed to be where you are, for nothing. Steve's advice for these hard times is to remember that the world moves on. No matter how tough it gets, get back up, brush yourself off, re-align your focus and hit it harder than before.

Ben Jaderstrom

Some people find their passion early in their careers and that has a remarkable effect on how quickly they become an Elite salesperson. During university, Ben Jaderstrom, when not hiking the mountains of California, surfing the waves and, when the snow came, hitting the slopes, had an interestingly entrepreneurial start to his career.

Ben loves music and throughout growing up, he was the person people would come to for recommendations, so he started a music blog. It appears it wasn't just his friends who appreciated his taste. At its peak, 25,000 individuals per day visited his blog to read his recommendations and had a popular Facebook page too. This is a serious amount of traffic! He made revenue from merchandise and advertising and had over 500 campus reps representing his brand. It was quite a different part-time job than most of his peers at university had.

After graduating, Ben decided that this wasn't how he wanted to build his career and instead hoped to join an organisation where he could learn.

Ben was well aware of the rapid shift from traditional ads to Facebook ads. He placed his bets and decided that this would be where he should focus his career. A digital marketing agency in San Diego produced exceptional results for their clients by leveraging a social advertising management tool called Social. com. They snapped up the opportunity to hire a guy like Ben.

His role was to optimise clients' campaigns to generate the highest return. Eight hours a day, locked in a room, he crunched numbers. Ben's energy comes from social interactions, and as he rarely had any client interaction, this role drained him. Ben prepared for a change of jobs.

During university, Ben and a friend dreamed of moving to San Francisco. His friend made the move ahead of him, which was a risk at the time, but he just went for it. This same friend had contacts within Salesforce and learnt that Social. com, a Salesforce division, was hiring, so he connected Ben with them. Social. com was achieving rapid growth and needed a person like Ben to manage their clients, one of which was his current employer. Despite his young age, his experience and depth of knowledge was second to none. He quickly secured the role.

They say the drive up the Pacific Coast Highway from San Diego to San Francisco is one of the most scenic routes in North America. It was a fitting journey for Ben to begin this next chapter of his life.

One of the biggest challenges tech companies face with new hires is ramp-up time, which refers to the time it takes for someone to be fully productive. As Ben was already an expert with Social.com, from day one he could advise his clients how to get the most from it. His clients loved him, and Salesforce took note that his clients' usage of the platform steadily increased with Ben as their account manager. This might have been one of the fastest ramp-up times Salesforce had ever seen.

Sometimes clients didn't have the internal resources to get the most from the tool, despite their best intentions. Ben proposed to Social.com management that they should start a managed service. Not only did they do this—they let Ben lead it. It worked so well that clients who used Social.com's managed service, compared with in-house teams, generated higher returns from their social advertising campaigns.

There were few people on the team with Ben's knowledge, such that the sales team were bringing Ben to meetings, to build credibility. Clients could instantly relate and trust him. This was a man who knew what he was talking about and who could help their business make social advertising successful. This helped secure many new high-profile clients.

As a sign of their gratitude, Ben was showered with gifts from the sales guys, comprising Amazon vouchers, football tickets, crates of wine, and so on. He soon realised that the sales teams were making tens of thousands of dollars a month, on the back of the six-figure deals he was helping them to secure. As much as Ben enjoyed receiving gifts and helping the team to succeed, he questioned his role. He concluded that if he added this much value to the sales team, why not join it?

Salesforce Marketing Cloud had just launched a new product called Active Audiences. The management team was the same as Social.com and they sought new salespeople to take it to market. Ben put himself forward.

Active Audiences took advantage of an innovative development by Facebook and Twitter. For the first time, brands could upload lists from their CRM to the social advertising networks. This meant that they could target or exclude people in these lists. When an advertising campaign is powered by CRM data, advertisers can expect a boost in performance. The problem is scalability. Advertisers have to manually upload CRM lists to the ad networks and refresh them regularly. If they do not, they risk targeting people at the wrong time with the wrong message, which has an adverse effect on campaign performance. CRM-based advertising campaigns require fresh data. In reality, most advertisers cannot commit the resources to do this and struggle to take advantage of the opportunity.

Active Audiences allows brands to power CRM-based advertising campaigns at scale. The product is a secure API between Salesforce Marketing Cloud and the ad networks, so lists are always up to date. Because of the simplicity of the product and the tremendous opportunity it allowed, demand for the product was hot!

Despite Ben's little sales experience, the knowledge he held and the relationships that he had established in Salesforce put him far ahead of the senior salespeople applying for the role. There was a long line of people queueing for this opportunity: salespeople with ten years' sales experience, closing big six- or seven-figure deals and overachieving target year on year. Yet management believed in Ben, so they took a risk and gave him the opportunity. As you can imagine, Ben's San Francisco dream was now really starting to take shape.

Given a sales target larger than some of the most experienced salespeople, Ben realised he needed to develop his sales skillset. This was the challenge he sought! In large corporations, complex solutions involve multiple salespeople. Active Audiences was part of the Marketing Cloud stack and Ben's role was to be a specialist within that team. They aligned him with almost 100 Marketing Cloud Account Executives. The workload was significant! First, he had to educate the entire team on the product and how to collaborate for success.

Quickly his diary filled. Some days he would have more than eight demos to perform for a product that averaged $40,000 a year. That's $320,000 of pipeline development per day. The high volume of sales opportunities and his close collaboration with 100 plus Elite salespeople was the perfect combination for fast development. Ben learnt from every sales engagement. His colleagues helped him to improve his sales skills across the board and his sales numbers demonstrated it. The intensity of his first year in sales was what many would have experienced in two or even three years.

Ben's exposure to some of the best salespeople in the industry—and a hot product that prospects needed—led to him becoming one of the top performers globally. In his first year of sales, he joined the Elite. Most are lucky to achieve even a marginally comfortable lifestyle in their first year in sales, but Ben purchased a house!

After his first year he needed a bigger challenge, as did Salesforce. Krux, Gartner's No.1 DMP (Data Management Platform), was acquired. This platform allows brands to unify data from their CRM, website, and ads (on publisher websites) to create a single customer view. In addition, it allows them to buy data from other providers, so they can enrich what they know about their customers and prospects. These clever capabilities allow brands to target the right person on the right channel at significant scale.

With an AOV (Average Order Value) of $250,000 a year and most clients signing multi-year contracts, it required a much more complex sales cycle. With this in mind, Salesforce merged the Active Audiences sales team with the Krux sales team. Ben received the next challenge that he had been seeking. Overnight, Krux's sales team had doubled. Training this many salespeople on a complex product was no straightforward task and many went without proper training for over two months. Ben addressed this by spending a lot of time with the Krux solution engineers and account executives to learn everything that he could. Without a pause, he chipped away at his number. Deal after deal he pushed ahead, finishing his second year in sales as the No. 1 global salesperson, against some of the best in the industry. He qualified for Presidents Club and was rewarded with a large pay rise.

Year three wasn't much different, yet this time there was no ramp-up time and Ben went straight into closing deals; however, his target was higher. Again, he was crowned the No. 1 global salesperson in the company.

Despite this, a nagging feeling returned. Despite the success, he no longer felt challenged, which had been his motivation to succeed. Once again, Ben evaluated his options. Because of his success, he found that many salespeople turned to him for advice and he enjoyed helping them to develop. Salesforce's rapid growth meant that they required new sales leaders. This opportunity appealed to him and he put himself forward.

At 29, Salesforce promoted Ben to Regional Sales Director, possibly the youngest ever in that company. He has achieved a lot in his short career to date. Personally, I'm excited to see where Ben takes his career next!

_____ **Ben Jaderstrom's sales career wisdom** _____

1. Become an industry expert.

2. Surround yourself with successful people, learn what they do and how they do it.

3. Practice makes perfect. Start with small business sales to drive high volumes which allows you to refine and improve your sales skills before you progress on to enterprise sales.

_____

It's rare for someone to achieve such rapid success in such a short period of time. Considering he entered his sales career as a specialist in a hot space, Ben fast-tracked. Most sales professionals find their expertise as they progress in their career.

Jon Levesque

Meet Jon Levesque, from northern Canada, whose warm smile instantly makes you feel at ease. Raised in a traditional blue-collar family, he learnt that if you want something, you must go and earn it yourself.

For Jon, that was computer games. He loved playing them, and so did his friends. Determined, he took on all the hustles he could as a young boy. The paper round, shovelling his neighbours' drives when the snow came (which is a big deal in northern Canada!) and mowing lawns when spring came. Whatever, however, Jon was there. It meant that he never missed out on having the latest computer games.

To pursue his passion for commerce, he studied business at university and, after graduating, started his career as a debt collector. Despite earning relatively little, he lived with friends, hung out with them after work, drank beer and remembers splendid times. It wasn't long though until his ambition kicked in, making him strive for more.

A friend of Jon's was becoming successful at Softchoice, then a billion-dollar organisation that was primarily a B2B software reseller. Excited about the possibility of entering tech sales and mirroring his friend's success, Jon eagerly asked for a recommendation. Jon's potential impressed Softchoice and they soon offered him a role.

This company had a defined linear career path, which made it easy for Jon to set his targets for the top. His first position was an inside sales role where he booked meetings for seniors and secured smaller transactional deals. Quickly proving himself, he became an account manager focussing on upselling and cross-selling existing accounts, which is where Softchoice made most of its money. Jon shadowed the most successful salespeople and continuously improved his calls, so he progressed at a rapid pace.

Softchoice set their eyes on New York to continue their rapid growth. Now with a track record, Jon put himself forward. At first the promotion was glamorous, yet he had to sleep on the floor of his New York apartment for three weeks, until his belongings finally arrived. Luckily it was only a short-term hiccup.

Focussed on expanding Softchoice, his remit grew to cover new business. For two years in a row, Jon was the No. 1 rep and attended Presidents Club with his fellow top performers. He was earning fantastic money while living in New York, which was a lot of fun!

Softchoice was growing so rapidly it couldn't hire salespeople fast enough. The biggest challenge was the nine-month ramp-up time. Impressed by Jon's success, they offered him an opportunity to move back to Toronto and teach the recent hires best practice, which he accepted. Jon reduced the ramp-up time to six months, which had a significant impact on revenue. To Jon's pleasant surprise, he found that, when he taught other people, his own sales skills improved too.

However, he missed the constant beat of new business. Jon became eager for a fresh challenge and to push his career even further forward. His previous manager from New York had moved to Softchoice's primary competitor, SHI International, and wanted Jon to join him, offering a position which would require him to open and lead an office in Virginia. The opportunity was too exciting to refuse; he accepted and packed his bags.

Virginia had a base of $5m in annual revenue. In only three years, Jon led the business to $65m in revenue, with plenty of growth on the horizon. Alongside this, Jon's personal life was also at an all-time high. He and his wife were ready to have their first child, although they decided that Toronto was a much better place for them to build their family. Jon handed over the reins and headed back to Canada.

Jon took some time to figure out the most effective way to progress his career. He had achieved an impressive amount of success working for resellers, who took a commission from vendors. Jon would then take his commission from the commission. Prospects often already knew what they wanted to buy, in which case Jon would simply fulfil the order. He decided that, if he could get into consultative sales and work directly for the vendor, that would propel his success.

This move meant that he'd step out of management and back into a role as an individual contributor. From a financial perspective, he realised that selling enterprise software for a vendor paid just as much, if not more, than being a sales leader at a reseller.

BMC Software, a company that develops core IT management software, was achieving rapid growth, particularly in the data centre space. The rapid pace of cloud computing had increased the demand for data centres and, as a result, the software required to maintain them became very lucrative. As Jon had resold BMC previously and was well versed in the space, he quickly secured the role.

The calibre of salespeople was something that he hadn't seen before and the sales leaders in the organisations knew exactly what they were doing. Rather than 'box shifting', Jon had to learn the full sales process and how to build value within it. Suddenly he felt out of his depth. He turned to relentlessly studying and shadowing his peers, which eventually paid off in terms of success.

Constantly being challenged, upskilling and working in a space that excited him, Jon spent five years with BMC, which were some of the most defining in his career to date. Towards the end of his time at BMC, he noticed the runaway success Datadog had been achieving in the U.S. They had secured major venture capital (VC) investment, rapidly grown revenues, secured huge logos as clients and built a world class sales team. Jon couldn't help but follow their success.

Datadog had developed a SaaS-based data analytics platform to monitor cloud applications such as servers, databases, tools and services. The value was instantly clear to Jon as he had spent the past five years deeply understanding clients' IT set-ups. So, when Datadog launched into Canada, Jon quickly applied. He knew this was a rare opportunity to secure major logos for a hyper-growth SaaS business.

To put this into context, imagine you are an ice hockey player. What is a sure sign that demonstrates you are one of the best players? Trophies! In the National Hockey League (NHL) there are upwards of 18 trophies and awards, and at the time of writing, they range from individual performance on and off the rink to team awards.[1] For salespeople, major logos are considered trophies.

There is an American football analogy that resonated with Jon when exploring Datadog, namely that of coaching trees. This means that the best managers breed the best managers. The Chief Revenue Officer of Datadog built his sales career at PTC (Parametric Technology Corporation), which is renowned for developing the highly effective MEDDIC sales qualification method.[2] Not to mention their outstanding sales culture. After creating MEDDIC in the '90s, PTC achieved 40 consecutive quarters of growth, which grew their $300m ARR (Annual Run Rate) organisation to over $1bn in just three years. MEDDIC is now used at leading organisations such as Salesforce, Oracle, Microsoft, Google, Autodesk and many more. The sales leaders who had built PTC and then left to join other organisations, as is normal in the world of work, individually built leading sales organisations. Dan Fougere, who became the Chief Revenue Officer of Datadog, was amongst them.

Jon was sold on Datadog and they on him. Datadog had a slick on-boarding process and an effective way of selling their tech, so Jon absorbed all of this knowledge and was quickly up and running. The buzzing culture of Datadog excited him daily and chasing down the big logos even more so. By the end of the first year, he'd played a major part in putting Datadog on the map in Canada. Datadog's revenue and headcount doubled for three or four years in a row, with a relentless pace, leading them to hire a country manager for Canada, to whom Jon reported.

This explosive growth made Jon stop and think about his own career trajectory. A company like Datadog propels you. He had achieved incredible success as an individual contributor and a proven sales leader. To progress at a faster pace in his own career, he believed the best thing to do would be to join a smaller organisation as a sales leader ready for hyper-growth.

In search of the right company, he found Densify, a SaaS company focused on the cloud tech stack, looking into data and scalability to reduce costs. Their offering did not compete with Datadog, and differed from BMC, but was firmly in the same space, making Jon's expertise a good fit.

With just over 100 employees and a fast-growing client base of impressive logos, Jon felt that Densify was really going somewhere. To scale growth, they needed a sales leader to build out the sales process and grow revenues, as well as build and lead a new business team. This was exactly the opportunity he had in mind and, after an intense interview process, Jon made the move, despite the huge potential still at Datadog. It was a hard decision, but Jon focussed on the bigger picture.

During my interview with Jon, he hadn't been in the role for long and was building the team. On the wall in the background was a poster for MEDDIC. No doubt Jon will achieve the success he desires in this role. Once he has ridden the wave with Densify, he can see himself joining an even smaller company, getting closer to the beginning of the journey, ahead of enormous growth.

When Jon reflects on memorable deal losses, he can attribute almost all of them to when he hadn't properly followed the sales process. It creates too much risk. His advice to all salespeople is learn the process and follow it, because it's there for a reason.

--- **Jon Levesque's sales career wisdom** ---

1. Become an expert in what you do and commit to excellence.

2. Put time on the bike. You cannot escape the value of experience.

3. Never stop learning and accept change.

SUMMARY OF CHAPTERS 1 TO 4

Let's take the opportunity to reflect, now that we've heard some interesting stories from some exceptional people.

Mandy Smithson and Ben Jaderstrom both deeply immersed themselves in the advertising sector at a time of tremendous digital disruption. The demand for adtech solutions skyrocketed and the complexity of the solutions was immense. What enabled both Mandy and Ben to achieve impressive success in sales was their industry expertise. It allowed them to build trust with their clients and secure their business.

Ben Tunstall has demonstrated character by building industry expertise in two industries and now transitioning to a third. First, he developed his expertise in mobile phones as the shift happened from landline phones. Good Technology, a mobile security vendor, was his first enterprise software sales role and although a hard first year, he developed his sales skills and earnt good money. Next he became a software sales recruiter, which is exactly the expertise LinkedIn required for their new business sales team, and joined upon their meteoric rise. LinkedIn accelerated the trajectory of Ben's career; he developed world-class enterprise sales skills and built a deep understanding of data. After several years, despite earning £300,000+ per year, Ben was no longer challenged. He scouted the market for the next big shift, which he believed would be in data and cloud computing, which is when he met and joined Snowflake. A tough transition, but the right move. All of the building blocks of Ben's career prepared him for his next moves to remain firmly in the heart of the action.

Steve Mason took a different approach. He gained deep experience within the sector of health and life sciences. His industry insights allow him to deeply understand the challenges his clients face, what motivates them, and where the industry is headed. This level of knowledge earns him the status of a trusted advisor, time after time. When someone specialises in a particular space, gains deep domain knowledge and focusses on a solution that solves a big problem when the market is ready for it, success quickly follows. These are two closely linked pillars of an Elite sales career: heart of the action and industry expert.

To become that person takes commitment and time. But it has to go beyond the financial gains. This has to be something you are genuinely passionate about, otherwise, to be frank, you just won't care and it will show. You need to love what you do.

Did you complete the exercise at the end of the previous chapter? Do you know which space you will focus on?

If you do, fantastic, continue with this chapter now. If not, I highly recommend you complete the previous exercise. To get the most from this, it's key that you know where to focus. You'll thank yourself, trust me.

Placing yourself in the right industry on your terms is a step in the right direction. Joining an established company with excellent training is the next step. Most sales organisations understand the importance of on-boarding new hires. The more effectively you train your staff, the quicker they will be effective and deliver their sales targets; it's as simple as that. As part of this training, often you'll learn about your industry, your competitors, why your products are the best fit and you'll complete sales training. At the very least, on completing this training, you will be able to move to a position where you can operate in your space.

Note also that Elite salespeople understand that on-boarding and working for a great company is just to get you to the starting line. To truly become an expert and elevate your success, you need to go deep. Here is some practical advice on how to develop deep commercial insights on your terms:

- **Read**: publications, case studies, reports etc.

- **Learn** from experts in your business: colleagues, consultants, clients etc.

- **Immerse yourself**: attend industry events, go to networking events, take industry/product-related courses.

Honestly, it's really not that difficult and nor should it be. The tough part is committing to doing it, to constantly learn and develop. This is what the sharpest minds do.

A constant focus is important. Take your time to map out a plan on how you'll do some of the above or other activities. This will help you not only to develop your deep commercial insights, but to continually sharpen them.

It's very important that this is your plan and that you enjoy it. That is how you ensure you stick to it and it becomes a habit.

When this happens, you'll be well on your way to becoming an industry expert, being viewed as a trusted advisor by your clients and, soon enough, outperforming your peers.

CHAPTER 5

STUDENT
OF SALES

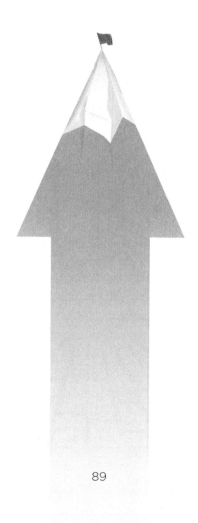

After education, many people are excited to finish their studies and start their careers. Time to make some money!

The reality is that your education has only just begun. In many professions, be it accountancy, legal, healthcare, software development, surveying, architecture, and others, there is a defined path of continuous professional education that naturally elevates you in your career as your knowledge builds. So why would the sales profession be any different?

The vast majority of people in sales stumble into the career and, as a result, that approach can shape people's philosophy on personal development. A fun question to ask any successful salesperson is 'how did you get into sales?' The answers are nearly always different, fun, and unexpected in their own right.

Compare that to doctors, lawyers or accountants and their answers are likely to be the polar opposite. From a young age they would have chosen that profession and studied hard to land a job in the best company they could. In sales, there is no true equivalent path. You can see why, for a long time, many had not perceived sales as a professional career.

I'm sure many parents over the generations skipped a heartbeat when their child reached the stage to build their career and said, 'I'm going to be a salesperson', rather than 'I'm going to be a doctor'.

This issue has been a challenge for a long time. A group of sales managers in 1911 decided that enough was enough. Their aim was to elevate the sales profession and to do so they formed the Sales Managers' Association. At first the

Association encompassed a monthly meet up, however, it emerged that this alone was not enough to elevate the profession. To step it up, they developed sales training courses that would grant their students recognised qualifications. As a result, membership grew rapidly and branches opened internationally. The Association even gained recognition by Prime Ministers and royalty. For example, in 1973, Margaret Thatcher, a Member of Parliament in the U.K. (later to be Prime Minister), endorsed the Association's 'year of selling', which led many companies to have record-breaking years in sales.[1] Without a doubt, this organisation has helped to elevate the profession.

However, a never-ending debate has plagued the Association, centring on whether sales and marketing are in fact the same profession. At several points, the Association's name included both marketing and sales in the title. Heated debates amongst senior members began, which led to fractures within the Association. So much so that spin-off associations formed and the name changed several times. Eventually sales and marketing went on their own individual paths. In 2016 the Association finally settled on the title the 'Institute of Sales Management'. Whether that settles the feud, only time will tell.

Which is exactly the problem. Despite the Association's best efforts, including the exceptional things they have done for the sales profession, the lack of solid foundations and continuous forward motion in harmony with their members prevented them from establishing an association with as much credibility as the likes of the ACCA for the accountancy profession.

To address the gap, many sales professionals have stepped up over the years to write books and share their knowledge on how to sell effectively. Several have created sales training organisations and the more successful ones have developed methodologies.

In the 1960s, Xerox corporation, whose primary business line was printers, lost market share to their upcoming competitors. As a result, their share price declined. Xerox had no groundbreaking product innovations in the pipeline to counter their competitors. Instead, they turned to sales.

Xerox invested millions in research to develop an effective sales system, which worked so well that, not only did they regain market share and increase their share price, they formed a sideline business to teach other companies this sales system (although I'm sure not to their competitors). 'Solution Selling' as it later became known, was the first complex commonly used sales methodology. Yet before this there are some interesting stories.

John H. Patterson, founder of National Cash Register (NCR), developed a sales system called pyramid selling in 1886. He taught salespeople to sell to the most important person in the business and have them win over others in their organisation. This method has become ingrained in the sales profession.[2]

Psychology increasingly became a focus over the years. A forerunner to the modern discipline, now largely discredited, was the phrenologist Grant Nablo, who in 1918 published his work proposing that the size of someone's forehead determined whether they were open to new ideas. The larger the forehead, the more open to ideas he claimed they were.[3] Ford Motor Company cars trained their sales team on this methodology. No wonder car salespeople get a bad reputation, and if you see a car salesman look above your eye line, you now know why!

Dale Carnegie released his all-time best-selling personal development book in 1936, *How to Win Friends and Influence People.*[4] The book has sold more than 15 million copies worldwide. Carnegie brought in a new era of relationship-based selling approaches that went beyond the trickery and deceit so many sales trainers taught.

From Carnegie, fast forward to the 1960s after Xerox released 'Solution Selling',[5] and thousands of salespeople had learnt this approach. It elevated the profession. Experts built on top of these systems in areas such as questioning, strategic selling and more.

Most notable is SPIN selling, which was developed by Neil Rackham in 1988, and published in a book of the same name.[6] Neil and his team listened to thousands of salespeople's calls, to understand what distinguished the Elite from the others. They found that questioning was the major difference. With this research, he constructed a process that became, and still is, highly effective:

1. Situational questions

This refers to understanding the prospect's situation. Elite salespeople keep this to a minimum and instead confirm the pre-research they did ahead of the call.

Situational questions rarely add value to the conversation; however, showing that you've done your research shows that you value their time.

2. Problem questions

This is the starting point of any sales engagement and often the reason prospects will engage with you in the beginning.

For example, maybe they have a very manual process that they want to shorten to reduce costs, or perhaps they are looking for a new supplier as the current one is failing to meet their standards? There are many other problems specific to industries and prospects.

Yet a problem question can rarely go beyond their most immediate problem.

3. Implication questions

This is where things get interesting, as they reveal the actual problem, not the cause of the problem.

For example, an increase in unit cost by 15% would be a problem, because perhaps the company is using an old machine. The implication is that the prospect has less profit to invest in growing the sales team, and as a result are losing market share to the competition. Thus, share price is declining, which is tied to the CEO's bonus, and resolving it is a priority.

4. Needs pay off

If unit cost can be reduced with an investment in the latest machinery, they can in turn invest the additional profit to expand the sales team, grow market share, increase stock price, and keep the CEO happy.

This is the premise of SPIN Selling: Situation, Problem, Implications and Needs pay off. It's hard to learn this approach naturally, but when you do, you will position yourself as more of a consultant than a salesperson. There are very few approaches that have mastered questioning in complex sales as effectively as SPIN.

Huthwaite International, the creators of SPIN, have achieved astronomical success in the sales training industry. Tens of thousands of salespeople have learnt SPIN. It is one of the most widely used sales methodologies and remains just as relevant today as it was in 1988.

A more modern sales methodology is the Challenger Sale, created by Matthew Dixon and Brent Adamson. The book of the method was published in 2011.[7] As with Carnegie's and Rackham's work, *The Challenger Sale* was written after a research project that yielded interesting results.

CEB (Corporate Executive Board), who were later acquired by Gartner in 2016, assessed thousands of salespeople across multiple organisations to understand what sets top performers apart from core performers.[8]

They uncovered five profiles.

HARD WORKER

- Always goes the extra mile
- Self-motivated
- Interested in feedback and development

CHALLENGER

- Always has a different view of the world
- Understands the customer's business
- Loves to debate
- Pushes the customer

RELATIONSHIP BUILDER

- Builds powerful customer advocates
- Generous in giving time to help others
- Gets along with everyone

LONE WOLF

- Follows their own instincts
- Self-assured
- Independent

PROBLEM SOLVER

- Reliably responds
- Ensures that they solve all problems
- Detail-orientated

Across each profile is the combined make-up of a successful salesperson. To be categorised in one of these profiles means the traits you show are most closely aligned with that certain profile.

For example, you could be a Problem Solver, yet still have traits from the Relationship Builder and Hard Worker profiles, but overall the profile that describes you best is Problem Solver.

Table 2 shows how they stack up.

Table 2: The five profiles of top performers compared with core performers

PROFILE	CORE PERFORMERS	TOP PERFORMERS
Hard Workers	22%	17%
Challengers	23%	39%
Relationship Builders	26%	7%
Lone Wolves	15%	25%
Problem Solvers	14%	12%

The contribution is a credible and fascinating insight based on rigorous research, which makes sense when you consider modern selling. Because of digital touchpoints in business, 57% of B2B buyers are halfway through the sales process before they contact a sales rep. To set yourself apart as a seller has never been more difficult.

Challengers are experts, they understand their market, the problems clients face, and how to solve them. When they engage with clients, they focus on commercial education to challenge the conventional way of thinking. This allows them to build credibility and gain trust. CEB believe that Challengers are not born, they are made. Beyond their best-selling book, which sold over 500,000 copies, they built a highly successful sales training practice. Organisations such as Xerox, Siemens, SAP and many more have hired CEB to train their sales teams to become challengers.

Although for reasons of space I can only mention here a handful of methodologies, there are many more that are highly regarded, as well as countless insightful sales books. Yet there is no standardised way of learning to become an Elite salesperson; the education process is still very much in your own hands. So how do the Elite approach learning to be a salesperson?

Marcus (Last name concealed, upon his request)

Marcus's first key motivation in life was to make as much money as he could. English-raised, yet half Dutch and half Spanish, he came from a relatively poor background. To give himself the best start in life, he studied psychology at university.

After graduating, all his focus was on landing the best job he could. He met with a recruitment company and they saw enormous potential in Marcus. This company places graduates into entry-level sales positions and provides sales training. They are champions of the sales industry and have helped many to fast-track their careers. Marcus hadn't considered sales as a career, but became intrigued and met with several companies to explore the profession.

On this path, he secured a job as a product analyst for a major online marketplace. Before he accepted the role, the sales recruitment company put one last job in front of him, at a well-established Financial Services technology company, which we will call Finsda.

When Marcus stepped through the doors of Finsda, it inspired him. This iconic building is filled with the stories of major British businesses' success or failure. The hallways rang with this history. Unsure of what to expect, he was simply himself; the interviewers were impressed with his ambition, charisma, intellect and desire to learn. As the hour neared, Marcus told his interviewers he had to leave so he could be back in time for his cleaning job. That last sign of dedication secured him the role. Marcus was the youngest-ever salesperson Finsda had hired to that date.

The product was selling data and information services to stock market traders, and his key clients were trading firms. His task was to sell to highly successful people, with the goal of securing large contracts. Marcus truly found himself in at the deep end.

Fortunately, Marcus was surrounded by exceptional people, who were impressed by his willingness to learn and determination. They wanted to see him become successful. He had five or six mentors, whom he would quiz and shadow, helping him to learn the ropes.

There are several stories he remembers from his early days, and one tough meeting in particular. The highly successful CEO of one of their clients had a notorious reputation for having an aggressive temperament, and unfortunately for Marcus, he inherited the account. In his first encounter with the CEO, there were some issues to resolve. He entered the meeting room, which had a chair in the middle and the tables assembled around it. The moment Marcus sat on the chair, the CEO slammed his hand on the table, then he and his team unleashed a bombardment of tough questions, perhaps bordering on abuse, at the young man who sat in front of them.

Marcus remained calm and handled the situation brilliantly. Fortunately, he had the answers to their problems and carefully addressed them, one by one. The hostile environment cleared and the client became somewhat positive. Marcus could then turn the conversation into a sales opportunity. He gained an enormous confidence boost after this meeting. If he could handle this, he could handle anything.

DING, DING, DINGGG!!!

The sales floor roared as Marcus rang the sales bell securing his first deal, doing his mentors proud. Not knowing what to do next, one of them sat down with him to help process the contract, but they noticed the signature was missing... Marcus had assumed that a verbal yes from the client was a closed deal!

Fortunately, the signature came later that day. They still joke about this, many years on.

In addition to mentorship, Marcus studies two or three courses a year. The subject might span financial services, business, sales, psychology (Sigmund Freud and Alfred Adler, two of his favourites), or anything else that will help propel him onward. The interesting combination of continuing studies and mentorship has allowed Marcus to create his own unique style and sales system, taking the best from what he learns.

At 27, after more than 5 years at Finsda, he has achieved 180% of his number, year on year, and is one of the highest paid and youngest people in his team. The senior salespeople now come to Marcus for advice.

Marcus's sales career wisdom

1. Choose your mentors, shadow them and understand what it is they do to be successful.

2. Understand what success looks like, measure it and do whatever is required to stay on track.

3. Deeply understand your market and profession, commit to personal education.

A key part of achieving rapid success is being in the right environment at the right time. For some people like Marcus, Ben Jaderstrom and Joachim Haas, their first sales roles couldn't have been more fitting for one of these environments.

Brendan McLaughlin

Brendan McLaughlin's story begins in a different era, from humble origins in the small English town of Rugby, near Coventry. His father was a policeman and mother a nurse, and there was nothing Brendan loved more than playing football. For the love of sport, he wanted to be a professional footballer. Brendan is now in his fifties and nearing the end of his career. At the time he wanted to become a footballer, it really could only have been for the pure love of the sport, because when Brendan was a teenager, footballers were not the megastars they are today. One thing Brendan loved about playing football was that he found it was an economic leveller. When you stand on the field, no matter your background, you are equal.

As he finished his studies, he sustained an injury that took football as a career off the table, and the sales profession intrigued him. As with the football pitch, the opportunity to decide who you want to be and to be measured by your results excited him.

When Brendan started, print ads dominated marketers' spend and a leading car magazine, Automart, was hiring junior salespeople. Gradually learning his craft, achieving some success, he realised the product you sell has a big impact on your success. He turned his attention to the leading player, the *Yellow Pages*.

In 2019, the *Yellow Pages* is no thicker than this book, but many years before it was an icon. There was a heartwarming ad where a young boy, too short to kiss a girl, put the *Yellow Pages* on the floor, stood on it and kissed her on the cheek. Young boys of today will need to think of more creative ways to kiss their sweethearts.

Ad sales were ruthless, fast-paced and a lot of fun. They mainly targeted SMEs such as small law firms, accountancies, tradespeople, car garages and others. Town to town, door to door, you had one opportunity to close the deal; it was there and then, no excuses.

Yellow Pages had a culture of investing in their staff and developing top salespeople, so Brendan took it seriously. As a result, his commission pay-outs grew, he won numerous awards and was promoted to a first line manager. Feeling successful, making a modest income, it wasn't long before he was eager for a new challenge. The road trips across the country and long hours were starting to lose their excitement. He hypothesised that selling to larger businesses would mean a more professional environment, fewer hours and higher pay. His colleagues at the *Yellow Pages* thought he was crazy. Brendan dismissed their opinions and pushed on.

Advances in technology meant that phone systems were getting increasingly more effective and investment from businesses small and large surged. Brendan noticed this and focussed on the communications industry. He landed a job at a top player in the U.K., Martin Dawes Communication, which was later acquired by BT, before spinning off to a new brand, O2. His first role was to sell to mid-size corporates. First, he developed his skills for a more professional environment and complex product. After succeeding, he progressed his way up in management and ran sales teams before running the business unit that served the Police Force in the U.K. He grew that business unit from zero to over 26 Police Forces with a yearly revenue of multi-millions in just a few short years, and O2 became the No. 1 provider to the Police in the U.K.

Like the *Yellow Pages*, O2 believed in investing in its people, and as a top performer, Brendan received the very best training. Still to this day he claims not to have received better. They opened the doors for him and his peers to meet many business leaders and coaches, to broaden their skills as professionals. A few notable moments are when they met:

1. Sir Clive Woodward, the 2003 World Cup winning coach for the English rugby team and Elite performance coach for the British athletes in the London 2012 Olympics. He taught a handful of people in BT the importance of an elite, winning mindset.

2. The youngest ever SAS Captain, the most elite military unit in the world, taught them how to focus on only what matters.

3. Ranulph Fiennes, one of the world's most legendary explorers, who taught his concept of living life 'with no limits'.

BT exposed Brendan to inspiring people like this from all walks of life. It taught him invaluable lessons in both business and life.

As a result of deciding to invest in the excellent development on offer, over the years Brendan's success grew. Consistently he was in the top 5% of the company and won numerous awards, including the prestigious U.K. 'Best in Class' Strategic Development Director of all sales industries, awarded by the ISM (The Institute of Sales & Management). What he found more rewarding than the awards and recognition of his peers was the respect he earnt from senior police leaders, who would call Brendan unannounced to ask for help and advice on transformation projects such as 'customer service' or 'contact centre management'.

After 16 to 17 years in the telecoms industry, Brendan had worked for 6 or 7 companies through mergers, he had learnt innovative technologies, and had been on a non-stop rollercoaster. Yet after that amount of time, every day felt the same. He sought a more exciting challenge.

Brendan noticed how the back-office systems in organisations had developed and felt the space was heating up. He dug deeper and uncovered the world of ERP (Enterprise Resource Planning). Top ERP salespeople earnt more than senior leaders in his business. This motivated him to explore this career path. In this search he spoke with many organisations. Of all those he spoke with, he was most sold on SAP—and they on him. Brendan made the move from telecoms to ERP, to lead and grow SAP's police sales team. Having an established network in police forces across the country and being experienced in enterprise sales primed Brendan for success. The challenge was to learn 10,000 SAP product lines, which was mentally exhausting. Yet, committed to his success, he put in the graft and studied.

What really made it click was securing his first multi-million pound deal. In his first year he was a modest performer, in the second year, a solid performer, and by his third, one of the best in the U.K., winning the largest new landmark agreement in the public sector. Brendan had successfully transitioned to enterprise software sales. Oracle got in touch and offered him the opportunity to run their European public sector business. Brendan hadn't done international sales before; his career had solely been in the U.K. He saw it as a step up both for his career and finances, so he accepted.

On day one Brendan inherited an underperforming and understaffed department. His role was to develop a sales strategy, execute it and grow the team. Extensive travel across Europe was required and Brendan soon realised the importance of in-country salespeople. For the first time in his career, his success slowed, which drove him to push even harder. Gradually the pipeline grew and deals matured. Success was in sight, yet still not where he wanted it to be. Motivated to succeed, he continued to push towards his goals.

Brendan's previous leader at SAP, the director of U.K. public sector, had moved to a data security start-up and wanted Brendan on his team. To begin with Brendan couldn't accept, because he had to finish what he started. But then he received an offer he couldn't refuse. Despite wanting to get the ship back on course at Oracle, Brendan accepted the new role.

SAP and Oracle had given him a solid foundational knowledge of ERP, enterprise databases and cloud computing. This helped him rapidly learn the data security company's products, which immediately generated effective conversations with prospects. In two short years he had led the team to secure several new multi-million pound contracts in the public sector. Unlike Oracle, this company set him up for success. Brendan was back on top.

You can imagine that, by this stage, large organisations were almost entirely run on large software applications. Yet endless manual processes still plagued them. To address the problem, a new field of technology emerged, called Robotic Process Automation. This technology automates manual tasks to reduce costs and allow organisations to become more agile. It was a groundbreaking innovation that became one of the fastest-growing segments in enterprise software, and was quickly forecast to become a billion-dollar industry in its infancy.

UI path was founded in Romania in 2005 and was one of the key pioneers, raising over $1bn across several investment rounds, and being valued at over $7bn in 2019. At the time, 400,000 people used their technology and they had an impressive roster of enterprise clients. They sought a sales leader to secure large government contracts and reached out to Brendan as a potential candidate. It was like Marc Benioff of Salesforce reaching out to you near the beginning of their journey and asking you to lead one of his sales teams. Brendan made the move, knowing that this would be the next big wave.

No surprises about what happened next: Brendan secured numerous net new contracts in his first year. He credits success to the solid foundations that he has built in his career and determination to succeed, no matter the challenge.

Brendan is a sales veteran, and it was an absolute pleasure to hear his story. In the past 30 plus years he has seen old-school sales tactics of trickery and deception develop into highly consultative sales. Sales has grown into a profession to be proud of.

Brendan McLaughlin's sales career wisdom

1. Beyond all, be yourself, time goes by quickly, love what you do and don't pretend to be something you are not.

2. Appreciate those who help you succeed, mentorship and help from others is the number one driving force for success.

3. Hone your craft and take training seriously.

As Brendan has a few more years on his career than the majority in the research project, it seems only fair to include a bonus point.

4. Persistence & tenacity will always help you develop your skills to be more effective.

Justin Golding

Justin Golding is a prime example of someone who has honed their craft. He grew up in an English coastal city, Portsmouth, home to the British Navy, with salt in the air. He is no stranger to hard work. At 17, he dropped out of the education system and started a career in retail as a management trainee. Quickly he realised a career in retail meant long hours, hard work and very little money. His enthusiasm dwindled and he looked for an alternative path.

In Portsmouth, office space was relatively cheap and wages slightly lower compared to London, which meant several insurance companies had set up shop.

Working for an insurance company would offer Justin the opportunity to earn over £35,000 a year, which, in 2008, was a gigantic leap from £22,000 as a retail manager, so he applied for a sales role. It was rare for an insurance company to interview people so young, but this company loved Justin's work ethic and desire to succeed; they took a risk.

Justin stepped into a buzzing office in which 200 people were on the phone, pitching, striding up to the sales board, writing up their freshly won deals. He was pumped, yet slightly intimidated. Eager to get started, he shadowed the best people, got his head down during training, learnt the products and then got on the phone. It was a sink-or-swim situation, so Justin gave it his all and, in just a few short months, became the top insurance salesperson in the company. They'd never seen anything like it!

With some savings accumulated, and after a few years of graft, Justin desired an adventure. He left the insurance company on a high and backpacked around Australia for six months, partaking in endless wild adventures. Savings depleted, he headed back to the U.K. to top up his bank account and then head back out. In his job search, he came across a tech start-up in Portsmouth, Lead Forensics, that had just launched a groundbreaking website tracking tool that revealed the contact details of a business on clients' websites.

Paul Thomas, the Managing Director, was the first inspirational person Justin had met. Like Justin, Paul had also dropped out of the education system early. He had developed his sales and marketing skillset before founding the U.K.'s leading telemarketing agency with a friend. Before the age of 30, Paul and his friend were multi-millionaires. Impressed by Justin's early signs of success, Paul inspired Justin to think about his potential and that making some money and going back travelling would be an error. It didn't take much to convince him; he wanted to learn everything he could from this man.

Justin was one of the first five salespeople at Lead Forensics. At the time they were still trying to figure out how best to sell the product. The approach of beginning with a cold call, securing a demo, offering a trial and then closing, while running high volumes in the pipeline as the average order value of the product at the time was small, seemed to work.

Numbers ramped up, the sales team grew and competition heated up. Determined to stay ahead, Justin listened to his calls to understand what was working and what he could improve, as well as listening to his peers' calls to learn from them. Not only did he do this every morning, but for a period of time he also came into the office on a Sunday when nobody else was there except Paul Thomas. In addition, he read countless sales books, Zig Ziglar being his favourite author of all time. This hard work paid off. Justin's consistently outstanding performance impressed Paul Thomas and he was rewarded with a promotion. Justin took the reins as the Lead Forensics sales manager.

As the team grew, the company hired an additional sales manager and again competition heated up. This time, the prize for the winner was to launch Lead Forensics in the U.S.

One mistake new sales managers often make is to try to make their team clones of themselves, as Justin soon learnt. He focussed instead on understanding his team, their goals, what drove them and how to coach them to become themselves on the sales floor.

Lead Forensics hired people at the beginning of their sales careers and Justin's role as a sales manager was to train people from the ground up. Personal development became a daily activity for his team. Justin encouraged his team to listen to their calls, read sales books and shadow top performers. A lot of them couldn't hack this intensity—it was like going back to school, and they left. The ones that stuck it out became top performers and several were promoted to managers.

Justin's empowered team won the battle between the two sales managers. He would be moving to Atlanta with one of the top performers on his team and also a friend, an Irishman named Phil. They built a sales pipeline ahead of the move to prove that the model worked in the U.S. Within a few months they delivered their sales targets. Things were now real!

Building the team wasn't so straightforward. There really is a cultural difference and it took a good few months for them to hire the right people. Slowly but surely they found top talent, trained them and they delivered; the success in turn attracted success and the U.S. sales team rivalled that of the U.K.

Fast forward four years, and Justin had grown the team to 90 people, including customer success and support staff: he led up to ten sales managers and had two offices, one in Atlanta and another in Phoenix, Arizona. Paul Thomas had been right about Justin.

In his personal life, things were great too as he'd just got married and bought a lovely house. Though something was missing, and every day seemed the same as the others. He was no longer challenged.

Justin reflected on what he had achieved and was proud of his success. One thing he realised he hadn't really done was experience true enterprise sales. Sure, he'd won plenty of enterprise clients, but the biggest deal he'd closed at that point was worth £65,000. To step forward in his career, he needed to close big six- and seven-figure deals with large enterprise clients.

Above all, Justin wanted to test himself, asking himself whether he was operating at the most Elite level. What if he could surround himself with people who were better than him and then excel; surely that would be career advancement?

When researching the compensation enterprise account executives receive, it was about the same as his current position and with fewer working hours. He'd always dreamt of being able to walk his children to school in the morning. As a VP, that would be a fantasy. A move like this would mean that he and his wife could start a family, something they both wanted.

In a bold move for a manager of managers, Justin interviewed at several companies, securing a role at an enterprise web personalisation company, leveraging his experience in the space. Justin's decision devastated Paul Thomas. It wasn't an easy goodbye, yet Justin had to do what was right for him and his future family. He made the move.

After some time in the new role, to his distress, he was underperforming. His determination to succeed still firmly in place, he slowed down and took time to evaluate. The culture fit wasn't right and perhaps there were better companies for him. Now he found himself in a dangerous situation, not being successful at this company and moving to another might leave a nasty stain on his C.V. Whatever he did next had to be right.

Two promising tech start-ups, Outreach and SalesLoft, caught Justin's attention. They had experienced explosive growth as the demand for their products was hot! Their success had reached such a level that they'd created a new enterprise software category: sales engagement platforms. These platforms enable call recording for sales coaching, task automation and centralised sales assets. Justin knew this stuff inside out as a previous VP of Sales and he knew the impact it would have made at Lead Forensics.

After several interviews, Justin saw his future at SalesLoft and carefully negotiated an enterprise sales role with an excellent compensation package. Unlike his previous role, this time they set him up for success. The culture was a perfect match and the maturity of the market was just right. It was now down to Justin to deliver. Failure was not an option.

Reality hit, and being an individual contributor is hard. To build a pipeline from scratch in the enterprise space takes time. SalesLoft expected him to deliver revenue in the first three months.

Six months in, he had not closed any deals and his wife gave birth to their daughter. An amazing perk SalesLoft offer is six weeks of paternity leave for fathers, but Justin decided to only take one week as he wasn't happy with his performance to date. He had to grow his pipeline and close some deals or risk putting his career in jeopardy. Had he again made the wrong move?

He refused to give up and doubled down on sharpening his skillset. Going back to basics, he listened in to top performers' calls, reviewed his own calls, sought mentors and tapped into his network. By month eight, still no business. The pressure intensified!

One of salespeople's favourite sales tools is e-signatures, because before they existed, a buyer would mostly print the contract, sign it and then scan back a copy or, if the buyer was old school, you'd have to wait a few days for it to arrive in the post. E-signature tools allow contracts to be signed in minutes. They are a salesperson's best friend.

Nine months into SalesLoft, Justin received an expected notification from SalesLoft's e-signature tool, DocuSign. The decisionmaker for a deal he'd worked for seven months had just read the agreed contract, and twelve minutes later, the signed copy landed in his inbox. A few days later the process repeated for another deal he had been crafting.

In month nine, Justin landed two deals worth more than $200,000 apiece, which saved his career. Then the floodgates opened. Within twelve months he delivered over $2m in total business, was top salesperson globally for the quarter and only a few percentage points behind top for the year. Justin had learnt an immense amount throughout this period, tested himself and come out the other end, the Elite of the Elite.

Success doesn't mean he's taken his foot off the gas. He might have released the pressure slightly, but his intensity remains. Whether he remains an individual contributor, spending more time with his family or steps back into management, this time managing the Elite, time will tell.

Justin has shaped hundreds of salespeople's careers and I believe is well positioned to give advice to those who seek to join the Elite.

Justin Golding's sales career wisdom

1. Be in the right place at the right time. A company that's growing fast, in a hot space, that momentum will propel you.

2. Focus on developing your skillset as a way of progressing your career, don't fall into the trap of going into management too soon, progress into more complex sales first.

3. Be true to who you are, don't let organisations shape you into a robot. Yet don't let your ego impede personal development, it's important that you grow.

Marcus, Brendan and Justin have all had distinct paths from one another, yet all have ultimately developed the skillset of an Elite salesperson. When you take the time to understand people and explore what makes them successful, even though there are commonalities, you'll notice people are inherently different. What works for me might not work for you, and vice versa. You can't train salespeople as robots and perhaps that's why it's always been so difficult to create a sales association that stands the test of time.

SO, WHAT CAN YOU DO?

Learn, practise, review and repeat. I'm afraid there's no silver bullet. If you review the full skillset of an Elite salesperson, it is daunting, because trying to learn everything at once is an unrealistic task. Like any major task in life, break it down.

Here is an approach that you can apply at any stage of your career.

1. Learn

What skills do the most successful people in your current role possess? Not sure? Ask them! Three people is a good number to start with. No doubt you'll find commonalities in their different viewpoints. But don't just ask them what the skills are, ask them how they learnt them. Now, with a focus on what you need to learn, make a plan of how you can learn those skills.

First, rate yourself: what do you do well and what room do you have for improvement?

What can you do to master these skills?

Don't just keep this to yourself, run this plan past your manager or a colleague who has succeeded in your current role, such as the people you asked for advice on what it takes to be successful in the role.

Get their agreement on where you are today, where you're aiming to get to, and what your plan is to get there. It is your plan; you need to own it, but finding someone well placed to advise, and obtaining their view on the plan, will give you the confidence that this is the right plan.

2. Practise

Don't be afraid to fail by testing new approaches and new ideas; you need to push yourself outside of your comfort zone—it's at the core of any form of progression.

Trying things once or twice isn't enough; you need to run high volumes as that is the only way to master any new skill. That said, don't change too many things at once. If something is already working for you, continue to do that and make slight changes in the areas that you need to improve. Make small incremental changes often since that is the key to continuous improvement.

3. Review

To track that you've successfully implemented new skills, you need to measure them.

By working through the previous two points, you've already identified where you are today on the skills you need to learn, what you will do to improve and what success looks like, so the plan is clear.

An obvious measure is your sales numbers, which will be specific to whatever your company measures you on, such as meetings book, qualified meetings, X pipeline generated, X opportunities in negotiation, X revenue generated, X sales conversion, X AOV, etc. But it doesn't always measure whether you have learnt the skill.

Call recording is one of the most effective ways, if your company has it, and most do. Listening to your calls is a major commitment and something you should practise out of hours. Either before business hours or after, to maximise your time when prospects are active for actual sales. It's hard work, but your future self will thank you for this investment.

Be critical of yourself, identify what's working and what you could improve, notice the incremental changes you are making and keep track of your progress.

If your meetings are face to face, or there is no call-recording software, put some time aside to reflect on your meetings. Again, what worked well and what could you do to improve? This is best done shortly after the meeting, so it is still fresh in your mind.

4. Repeat

Keep going until you've mastered your role, are delivering your targets consistently, and have proven that you are a top performer.

The feeling you will have when you get there is one of the best. When you reflect on where you began and where you are now, it will fill you with confidence. You owned it, developed your skills and increased your value.

What's next?

Now that you have mastered your current role, identify what the next role should be, which you would have most likely already have done, and start understanding how to be successful within that role.

The task is the same: speak with three people who are already successful in that role, understand the skillset you must possess and the most effective way of learning it.

There is only so far you can go in learning these skills before you are in that role, yet there is always something you can do to prepare. For example, go and shadow some of your colleagues at meetings, to see for yourself first-hand what they do in action. Most people will say 'yes' if you ask them if you can shadow their meetings, you just need to ask, and asking is what most people do not do. If you show the hiring manager how you developed your skillset and how you've prepared yourself for the next role, it is a sure way to make yourself an obvious hire.

The beauty of this simple system is that it will work no matter how senior or junior you are in your career. To reach the top level of success in a sales career, you must build solid foundations that will support your personal growth. Year by year, you'll develop a well-rounded skillset and then, before you know it, you will become one of the people you moulded your success on. Make no mistake, this takes time and dedication. The investment you make in yourself will be one of the most rewarding you'll make in your career.

In support of learning the skills that you must develop, it's common practice for Elite salespeople to read books, listen to audiobooks, watch podcasts, follow sales blogs, take courses and other forms of personal development. Audiobooks and podcasts are good for those on the move. During your morning commute, do you listen to music, watch an episode from your favourite series, play a game on your phone, read the news, have a nap or just daydream? What if you turned that commute into valuable personal education time and prepared your mind for the day ahead? Let's just say your average commute is 45 mins, which is 15 hours a month assuming you travel in Monday to Friday. In that time period you could listen to/read at least a book a month or closer to one-and-a-half, which is between 12 and 18 valuable pieces of content you could consume to develop your knowledge and sharpen your skillset each year.

On your way home after a long day, I'd recommend not doing personal education. Your body and mind need an opportunity to relax, so treat yourself on the way home to your favourite playlist.

Reading a stack of books is not the aim. To say you read 20 books this year doesn't qualify for bragging rights. If you speed through a book and move on to the next, are you really going to keep that knowledge? The aim is to learn and apply the knowledge within; that is how you will gain value from this exercise.

You're far better off focussing on say eight books and applying the teachings to your career. Some content such as podcasts, fiction books, autobiographies and biographies can be sped through; they are a different type of content. Sales books need to be studied, the good ones at least. There is a lot of fantastic material out there and it's constantly growing, developed by people that know the challenges of this career and want to help others succeed. Consume it!

After a short while, this will become a habit, and when you see the results of putting this knowledge into action, it will only increase your motivation. The first step is to get started. What you're doing right now, studying this book, is a perfect example of that. For inspiration, there is a video channel on www.elite-salescareers.com where I have produced book reviews for those seeking to build their sales careers. Check it out!

In the meantime, here are a few highly regarded recommendations that will get you started on building your very own personal sales education library.

A SALES LIBRARY

Sales skills

Brent Adamson & Matthew Dixon *The Challenger Sale*

This is a modern classic that teaches you how to become a challenger, the most successful of all the sales profiles.

Neil Rackham *SPIN Selling*

Another classic, shared at the beginning of this chapter, which focusses on effective questioning techniques to build value in the sales process. This is a far more effective technique in complex sales as it would be over-kill in transactional sales and has the potential to be considered border-line hard-selling.

Many report that SPIN selling can be hard to learn and put into natural practice, but once refined, it becomes a very effective skill for any Elite sales professional. For those in complex enterprise sales, this is a must read.

Brian Tracy *The Art of Closing the Sale*[9] and/or
Zig Ziglar *Secrets of Closing the Sale*[10]

No sales library is complete without one or both of these sales legends, as very few others have championed the profession as much as these two. Be warned, they are old school and from a different era, so ignore that side of things. Their teachings are still just as relevant today. Both teach salespeople the behaviours of being a professional salesperson, how to act, how to think, how to speak and many more besides.

Brian Tracy is my personal favourite sales trainer of all time, and after reading *The Art of Closing the Sale*, I doubled my income in the twelve months that followed.

Classics on success

Some books seem to have stood the test of time. Often, they are based on research studies and, rather than focussing on methodologies, they focus on human behaviour.

Stephen Covey *7 Habits of Highly Effective People*[11]

Stephen Covey's best-selling self-improvement book and a classic that can be found on many successful people's bookshelves.

Covey studied successful people over many years and evaluated people's behaviours to form the 7 Habits of Highly Effective People. His teachings focus on developing the way you see the world and how you respond to it, with the aim of elevating your success. These habits must be practised and continually sharpened to master them.

It's an all-time classic and a must for anyone who is serious about personal growth.

Dale Carnegie *How to Win Friends and Influence People*

Dale Carnegie is one of the first notable authors to write about Emotional Intelligence. Decades on, his work remains relevant. Why? Because he focussed on human behaviour.

When you understand why people respond the way they do, it allows you to react carefully and build more meaningful relationships. The lessons within this book teach you how to be your best self when developing relationships.

Simon Sinek *Start with the Why*[12]

Simon Sinek's work has quickly become a modern classic, similar to Stephen Covey and Dale Carnegie. Sinek looks beyond what people do to why they do what they do. His teachings focus on business success and what separates leading brands from the rest. People don't buy what you do, they buy why you do it. In sales, we find ourselves in competitive environments daily. Sinek's teachings are a fantastic way to help us stand out from the rest.

Autobiographies and Biographies

There is a lot to learn from highly successful people's life stories. It is a superb way to draw inspiration, gather ideas and assess your own path. Their stories are often remarkable, which makes learning about them a lot of fun. No library is complete without a few big hitters.

For me to add key recommendations in this section I think would be unfair to all those incredible people out there; instead search for people who inspire you. Perhaps they are entrepreneurs, sportspeople or politicians? We all have someone who resonates with us more than others. When you find these people, learn about them. How did they achieve success? What makes their story remarkable? Draw inspiration from these people.

Financial Success

When those deals come in, learn to invest and build true wealth.

George S. Clason *The Richest Man in Babylon*

No success library would be complete without this. Written in 1920 by George S. Clason, the author teaches fundamental wealth-building lessons by way of the story of someone who lived in ancient Babylonian times.

His account is just as relevant today as it was back in 1920.[13]

Tony Robbins *Unshakeable*

Tony Robbins is another author who has published a modern classic. He interviewed 50 of the most successful investors around the world to understand their investment strategies and mindsets. With this knowledge he developed an investment strategy to create an 'unshakeable bank account', which he shares in the book.

Insightful and backed by highly credible investors, this is a fantastic read for those who seek to build wealth.[14]

Summary

One last piece of advice to leave you with is that when you speak with successful salespeople, ask them what books they recommend. We all seem to have a particular one or two that have affected us more than others.

Perhaps this book '*The Pillars of an Elite Sales Career*' will be that book for you? Or perhaps it is another one entirely.

What matters is that it influenced you and helped you to grow. The more you learn, the more you can earn.

CHAPTER 6

BE THE MASTER OF YOUR OWN DESTINY

A man without a purpose is like a ship without a rudder.

Thomas Carlyle

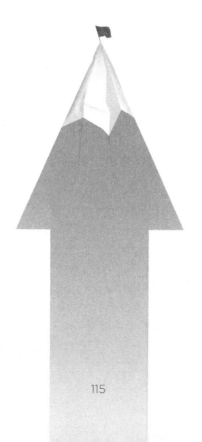

T hink back to some of the greatest explorers in history:

- Christopher Columbus, an Italian, famously discovered the Americas on behalf of the Spanish Catholic monarchs.

- Captain James Cook, the British explorer, led countless expeditions to discover Australia, New Zealand, Hawaii, Alaska and more.

- Neil Armstrong led the first ever manned expedition to the moon on behalf of the United States on the Apollo 11 spacecraft.

Had they just set off with no proper goal, do you think they would be in the history books? If your goal is to become an Elite salesperson, it is essential that you understand the path ahead to navigate your way to this prestigious place.

Before you embark on your journey, there are some variables to be aware of:

- The size of business that you sell to, including SMEs (Small and Medium Enterprises), mid-market and enterprise.

- The relative complexity of your product.

- Your role; lead generation, running and closing deals, managing client accounts and more.

- Whether you are an individual contributor or management.

To begin, let's explore the natural progression in the sales career path.

There's a lot to know about running a deal, from opening to closing and renewal. You can break it down into several roles.

The first role is the Business Development Representative (BDR) or Sales Development Representative (SDR) whose job is to generate sales opportunities. Day to day, they research accounts to form a sales approach and get in touch with prospects, usually via phone call, email or LinkedIn. They do whatever it takes to generate the opportunity.

Upon succeeding, the BDR/SDR arranges a call with the prospect to generate interest and qualify their need. Qualification is company specific, but it involves things such as whether the prospect has a relevant project, what budget they have, who the decision-makers are and more.

BDRs/SDRs then hand over the successfully qualified opportunities to the account executives/sales executives/business development managers, whose role is to run the deal to a close.

The complexity of the product and size of the business they sell it to has a large effect on the sales process ahead. As a rule of thumb, the smaller the business, the less complex the product, the shorter the sales cycle and the smaller the AOV (Average Order Value). Vice versa, the larger the business, the more complex the product, the longer the sales cycle, and the larger the AOV.

Small AOVs are usually less than £10,000 annually and these deals take a few months, a few weeks or even less time to close. Large AOVs are usually more than £100,000 annually, deals take over 6 months to close and can even run to 18 months or more, particularly when they are worth over £1m. While these statements are not always the case, it's a relatively safe rule to go by.

In SME sales roles, they expect you to close at high volume. In large business sales roles, the focus is on landing a handful of strategic deals. Salespeople naturally start with simple solutions before they progress to complex solutions.

High-value deals require a more mature skillset and it should come as no surprise that there is more revenue on the table. It follows that commissions for these deals are often higher.

Once a deal has closed, the after sales team takes over. This could involve client success, implementation or account management professionals. Again, this depends on the complexity of the product and the company structure. Complex products nearly always require an implementation phase. Finally, when the client is successfully up and running, it's an account manager's role to keep the client happy, secure any cross-sell or upsell opportunities and renewals. In some organisations, that entire role from opening to renewal can be just one person. By comparison, larger organisations tend to break it down so their salespeople can focus on the hardest part of the sales cycle, which is securing business. Which is also the role that pays the most. You will find Elite salespeople at the latter end of the spectrum. They secure large enterprise deals and expand their company's footprint within these accounts.[1]

As you can see, there are many variables to consider. Beware, some career progression paths can have a negative effect on becoming an Elite salesperson. Many believe that stepping into management is a career progression move.

As a successful BDR, your company may offer you a role as a BDR manager. This sounds great, but that career path can create difficulties for you further down the line. Without closing experience as an account executive, you could have a limited sales management career. To put that in context, let's say you become a highly successful BDR manager, progressing to become a senior manager running several teams and then eventually a global manager who runs the entire business unit. No doubt you'll have achieved some remarkable things, but where do you go from there?

It will be hard for you to manage and train quota-closing salespeople when you haven't done it yourself. OK, you might be a fantastic manager, but salespeople need managers who have been there and done that. Gaining the respect of your team is crucial.

Let's rewind. Maybe you decided not to become a BDR manager and instead you are promoted to SME account executive. Now is your time to shine and prove that not only can you exceed your targets generating meetings, but you can exceed your targets closing business. After two years of crushing it, being at the top of the game, receiving the admiration and respect of your peers, you're offered a role as an SME sales manager. Fantastic! With closing experience under your belt, surely now is the time to step into management. The career path to the top sales position, VP of Sales, looks a little clearer. Succeed at being a manager of quota-crushing salespeople, then become a senior manager, managing several managers, before reaching the top to lead the global sales organisation. This is a likely path, although certainly not an easy one. Having gained the experience of the full sales cycle, your management career will offer a lot more opportunities.

But there is still something missing. What about mid-market and enterprise sales? If you haven't built your experience there, are you in the best position to lead a global organisation that sells to mid-market and enterprise? Probably not.

You get the gist: if you want to make it to the top, avoid going into management too early. For longevity and adding maximum value to your sales career, prove your success in complex enterprise sales before stepping into management. Again, this is a general rule of thumb.

You might find that you're not a big fan of the long sales cycles, preferring the velocity of SME sales. That's not a problem, because you've got to find what works for you. The top of that career path still pays very well. A last path to be aware of is stepping out of new business roles entirely and remaining as an account manager. Elite salespeople close new business.

An exception to that lies in land-and-expand strategies. Sometimes with complex sales, we tackle a smaller part of the business, prove the success and upsell. This is most common with Global Account Managers (GAMs) or major account executives. As the title suggests, they work with the largest businesses in the world. Deal sizes are significant, take a long time to mature and a GAM will only have a handful of accounts, sometimes just one. This is the very top of the individual contributor path, and it's not uncommon for GAMs to earn over $1m in a strong year from commission. That said, with such a narrow focus, the role comes with more risk than other sales roles, which is why it is crucial to be at the top of your game before moving into such a role.

Finally, there is another role to be aware of, that of the channel manager/alliance manager. Earlier in the book, the concept was introduced in Ben Tunstall's story where he was tasked with developing partnerships whilst at Good Technology to generate pipeline. It is more of a strategic and support role in sales, yet when done well, it is a certainly a place where you find Elite salespeople. The same rules apply with SME, mid-market and enterprise sales, and sales management.

When you understand what the path ahead looks like as a sales professional, you can set your goals, learn the required skills to get there and stay focussed. The earlier you do this, the sooner your success will come.

Along your journey you may find that your existing company doesn't sell large complex enterprise solutions, making management the next step in career progression. When you reach that stage, assess the market and look beyond your own organisation. Your career progression is the most important thing, so think of your sales career as your own business. You call the shots.

Philip Nyborg

Philip Nyborg, from Denmark, is a prime example of someone who started his career with a clear direction. He always knew that he wanted to get into IT.

In Denmark, students are encouraged to work for 15 to 20 hours per week whilst at university and it's common practice for organisations to cater for this. IBM, the pioneers of the enterprise computing age, are big supporters. Phil set his sights on working for them and secured the role.

During Phil's five years at university, he worked in many departments, including accounting, marketing, sales and more. This gave him a solid understanding of how IBM operates. Above all, the people he met in sales inspired him. Phil wanted to be one of these people.

After graduation, there was only one thing he wanted to do, which was to work in sales at IBM. The way Phil looked at it, it seemed that IBM salespeople owned their own shops within the business. This excited him! As a driven individual, he loved how measurable it was. His already strong network in IBM meant the interview process was smooth. Globally, IBM is renowned for their exceptional sales training programmes. For the first nine months of the role, they give graduate salespeople no quota to achieve. Their job is essentially to learn how to be a successful salesperson.

First, they must make a territory plan for their assigned patch, ahead of an intensive five-week offsite somewhere in Europe. This includes intensive programmes to learn the products, the role, and a series of sales simulations with senior salespeople. There are five offsites in total and, to finish, a two-week sales masterclass. When you consider that, in many companies, on-boarding of new sales employees often comprises only providing a laptop, phone, some product training and introduction to their team, IBM's on-boarding is a whole other world. Not everyone passes, though. Those who do are finally contracted as an account executive and let loose to crush their target; those who don't are shown the door.

The majority of those who pass move into an inside sales role, which will typically involve smaller transactional sales to SMEs over the phone. Alongside this, they reserve a few roles to fast-track the most promising sales graduates directly into enterprise sales. Phil made it to the enterprise team to represent IBM Web-Sphere Software, which is IT infrastructure technology for integrating complex systems. To accelerate his career, he identified several successful senior salespeople, explained to them what he admired about their style and sought their mentorship. Not only was Phil able to shadow them in meetings, but if one of them was in the area when Phil had a meeting, they shadowed him.

Patience is mandatory in enterprise sales. Phil persevered with no closed business for the best part of his first year before closing a string of deals that pushed him through his target. Year on year after that, Phil crushed his sales targets, receiving yearly pay raises and promotions. This secured his position as an Elite salesperson.

Continuous personal development was key to his success. He attended industry events, read industry publications, completed sales courses and learnt IBM's new products inside out.

Several years into Phil's sales career at IBM, he again found himself at the sales bootcamp, this time as a mentor. His role was to evaluate new hires, share his wisdom and help them become successful. A proud moment. Seven years had passed and one of Phil's own mentors became concerned. He believed that if you spend too long in an organisation, it can give you tunnel vision and you only see the world the way your organisation does. This is a career limiting move, even if IBM's lens is powerful. The mentor advised Phil to look around. Funnily enough, SAP got in touch with him shortly after this advice.

Like IBM, SAP is a tech titan with a broad range of products. They had a position available to join their HANA division, which is a database management platform for advanced analytical processing, application development and data virtualisation. At IBM, Phil had specialised in cloud and big data related products, so this was a natural progression to help him build his knowledge. Throughout the interview process, Phil felt he could learn a lot at SAP. This move would force him outside of his comfort zone and SAP also offered an increase in pay. Phil made the move.

Dedicated to succeeding, Phil immersed himself in SAP's culture. He studied their proposition and identified several mentors to shadow. This shortened his ramp-up time and his sales success continued. What Phil found most exciting was the pace of the industry. Cloud was here to stay, data usage within organisations had exploded, and new use cases kept coming. Every year in the industry expanded his knowledge and strengthened his position as an expert.

Up to this point in his career, Phil had only worked at big corporates, and a few years after his success at SAP, Phil itched to join a hyper-growth start-up. Datadog, an IT application monitoring tool, had experienced an astronomic rise; their growth had exploded out of the U.S. and they had opened offices across

Europe. To launch into Denmark, they required a team of highly experienced experts. Datadog came to know about Phil's in-depth experience across IT infrastructure, big data, and his outstanding sales track record; they approached him directly to join their team. Intrigued by the opportunity, Phil conducted some thorough analyse and due diligence, after which he accepted their offer without hesitation. Within months of his start date he couldn't have been happier, because Datadog submitted an initial public offering (IPO) and fortunately for Phil he had secured some shares as part of joining the company. This really was the hyper-growth start-up he was looking for.

There are few people in their early thirties who have as much experience in enterprise sales as Phil. He started with a solid career plan and immersed himself in the right environments, and that allowed him to achieve rapid success. Through these experiences, his words of wisdom hold a lot of weight.

Phil Nyborg's sales career wisdom

1. Earn your spot in meetings, become an expert in what you do and always focus on adding value to your client.

2. Always push yourself and aim high. Great things do not happen in your comfort zone.

3. Understand what makes you tick, dig deep, connect with your passion and use that to drive you forward, it will allow you to become authentic. Authenticity instantly builds trust with clients.

Some of us begin our careers in less structured ways.

Hugh Darvall

Hugh Darvall, an Australian from Melbourne, started in sales straight after university. He graduated with what he calls a 'Bachelor of Attendance'.

Intrigued by the fast-paced environment of the events industry, he joined a company called Expo Hire that specialised in everything a business could need to exhibit at an event. Hugh's job was to secure new clients and upsell existing ones. One of the most rewarding things he found from the job was when a client's design came to life at the event. As fun as this job was, the pay was not fantastic. With an ambition to earn a lot of money, he learnt about a lucrative opportunity in software sales.

Hugh's first problem was that he had a very limited network in the software industry. To resolve this, he had a coffee with just about anyone who would speak to him in the industry, to make inroads.

Before long, Hugh was a borderline coffee addict and received an introduction that would change the course of his career. A young entrepreneur had founded a business called CMO Compliance that had developed a number of compliance-focussed best practice products. This entrepreneur was trying to find product market fit and needed salespeople. The two met for a coffee. Impressed by Hugh's proactivity and natural hunter-like mentality, he made Hugh an offer. Without hesitation, Hugh accepted and was ecstatic to start his software sales career.

At the time, Australia's mining boom was in full swing. The mines' growth meant opportunities for suppliers were plentiful. If you've ever spent much time in Australia, you'll see they are big on safety and a dangerous place like a mine is on the extreme side of that. The compliance standards are high and keeping on top of these can involve very manual and time-consuming tasks.

Hugh focused his efforts on the mining industry and quickly generated large opportunities. Mine to mine, department to department, they secured deals. As the company was a young start-up, Hugh had to do a lot more than sales. He got involved with client installations, interviews for new team members and even banking. All involved enjoyed this economic boom for several years, and life was splendid. But before long the mining boom slowed and the sales opportunities dried up. Hugh turned his attention to other sectors. Although he experienced success with other industries, it wasn't quite the same as it had been before. Hugh's enthusiasm dwindled and he searched for a new role. Up to that point he'd learnt that if you can solve large-scale, manual problems, it leads to big software deals. Hugh focussed his efforts on companies that did this well.

Employing shift workers creates a mammoth task for large employers; take the police for example. Each department will have thousands of employees working around the clock, so keeping on top of people's shifts requires a department in its own right. The manual aspects of doing this meant that it was expensive and full of inefficiencies.

Planning and scheduling software is big business as it automates much of the processes business must follow. A leader in the field, Quintiq by Delmia, was seeking new salespeople. The transition was a natural fit with Hugh's experience, so he applied and secured the role.

It took a long time to learn the complex product and the sales cycle was much longer than Hugh was used to. Delmia almost exclusively sold to large enterprises. As determined as Hugh is, he struggled to get into the tech and the sector really didn't excite him. He stuck it out for the best part of a year and then searched for another role. This next move had to be right. It was critical that Hugh got himself back on the success track to move his career forward.

At the time, the 2008 financial crisis had hit and Hugh started to fear that the world was against him. First the decline of the mining boom, followed by a move to the wrong company, and now businesses were not spending... what could go wrong next? In fact, the downturn created the big opportunity Hugh was seeking!

Software giants such as Microsoft, Adobe, SAP and many more all felt the impact of the financial crisis. It was industry wide. The decline in sales demand revealed an interesting way to make revenue, albeit, I'm sure, not popular one with clients. After several audits, software companies realised that many clients were overusing their software, which led them to make audits at random. If they found clients were breaking the conditions, they charged them large fines.

This wave of audits all seemed to happen at the same time and the time taken to audit internally was immense for users of the software. This gave rise to Flexera, a software asset management tool. Joachim Haas, mentioned in Chapter 3, had been in the same industry, leading the European arm of a competitor at a similar time. Flexera's success in the U.S. and Europe led to the launch of the Australian office in Melbourne, to serve as the base for Asia Pacific. They focussed heavily on partnerships to create sales opportunities and needed salespeople. Hugh eagerly applied. During the interview, the worldwide sales leader asked Hugh what his ambition in Flexera would be, to which Hugh replied that he wanted to run a region. Essentially Hugh said that he wanted his leader's job. Impressed by Hugh's track record and ambition, it was a straightforward decision. Hugh got the role and, along with it, a new mentor who wanted to see him succeed. Hugh's new boss gave him some advice that he's kept close ever since, which was, 'show your value'.

Without hesitation he learnt the product in-depth. In year one he built the indirect sales channel, which made a big impact on overall sales. By year two he had received a promotion by which he would also be responsible for renewals and the inside sales team. Continuing his trajectory, he showed success within the new role and alongside that Flexera grew. Initially they focussed on only large businesses, but they subsequently expanded to serve mid-market companies too. By Hugh's third year in the company, his remit once again expanded and he was now responsible for the channel, alliances, renewals, inside sales and mid-market.

Within a year it was clear to the business that Hugh had the potential to be the region's future leader, yet there was one thing missing: he hadn't had a great deal of experience in closing major enterprise accounts. Dropping his leadership position, Hugh took on 20 of the 40 top accounts and prospects for Flexera in Australia and New Zealand. Once again, he was an individual contributor and knew that if he delivered his number, he'd line up the position to run the region.

Enterprise sales takes some time, so he learnt all that he could from the existing key accounts manager and applied his newly found knowledge. Penetrating new accounts and upselling existing clients was his daily focus, and slowly but surely he built pipeline and started to bring in the business. Proving himself for another two years, Hugh's skillset was unquestionable.

Flexera had rapidly grown in the region, establishing itself in Australia, New Zealand and Asia, and Hugh had played a key role in their success. The management layer grew and the VP was ready to hand over sales leadership for Australia and New Zealand. Hugh was rewarded with the role he had sought from the beginning and was promoted to Director of Sales for Australia and New Zealand. This was the proudest moment of Hugh's career and he did exactly what was suggested to him from the beginning; he showed his value. There couldn't be a better example of someone setting a goal and relentlessly plotting their path towards it.

As exciting as success is, some people find it unfulfilling, because they realise that the journey is the reward. Hugh felt proud to run the region every day for two years and continued to achieve rapid growth, but after a while he started to seek his next opportunity, making an unlikely move.

Reflecting back on the mining boom and the initial boom in asset management software due to the financial crisis, Hugh kept coming across Datadog, as we have already seen in Chapter 4 with Jon Levesque. Amazed by their rapid rise, he learnt that they had launched in Australia and were on a path toward IPO. As a senior salesperson, fast-growth tech companies often offer options, which if they submit an IPO or are acquired, materialise as cash. The problem is that most won't, although Datadog seemed liked it might.

Unfortunately for Hugh, he had missed the opportunity to lead the region for Datadog, yet nonetheless he remained highly interested. Having already sold and engaged with the top accounts in Australia and New Zealand, servicing a similar stakeholder, there was a very clear fit. Feeling that there was no room for growth left at Flexera, he wasn't sure when a rocket ship like Datadog was going to come along again, so making a bold move, Hugh joined Datadog as an enterprise account executive for Australia and New Zealand. He was tasked with securing the largest accounts, which was one of the top positions in the team. Within a year Datadog had their IPO, so it was a solid move by Hugh.

There are few people as well rounded as Hugh, few who see virtually every aspect of sales.

───────────── **Hugh Darvall's sales career wisdom** ─────────────

1. Find a company you can be successful in and build on that success, stick it out and go as far as you can.

2. Personal development is key to getting ahead, take it seriously and learn the skills necessary to progress.

3. Sales is a rollercoaster of a career in which you will have your highs and lows. Don't let this affect you, it's important you have thick skin and remember to celebrate the good times.

───

In the sales profession we joke around that almost no one dreamt of being a salesperson when they were younger, but there are a few very rare exceptions to that.

Suzanne McGettigan

Suzanne McGettigan grew up in the large city of Mississauga, Canada, which neighbours Toronto, and at the age of twelve, she gained her babysitters' licence. She went from one house to the next, taking care of the Smiths' children, the Andersons' children, the Martins' children and many more, whilst their parents enjoyed much-deserved nights out to themselves. She was probably one of the highest-paid twelve-year-olds in her town.

At 15, Suzanne was friends with a young guy who worked in a radio station, interviewing all of the best music acts at the time. Suzanne's friend invited her along to watch their interviews, meeting the likes of big artists such as Soundgarden, Ozzy Osbourne, and Radiohead. The first thing she packed was her camera. One afternoon, she met Soundgarden and she took plenty of pictures to capture these moments.

Several months later, Soundgarden were playing in Toronto. She had a genius entrepreneurial idea that required some assistance, so convinced her best friend to join her and together they made preperations... They showed up at the gig, with no tickets. Suzanne and her friend had produced copies of the pictures she had taken of the musicians at the recording studio. She even had an old drumstick.

They walked down the queue, shouting, *'Soundgarden pictures for sale! Matt Cameron's drumsticks for sale!'*

Young girls and guys ran screaming at them: they fought over the original pictures, a back edition of the band on the cover of Rolling Stones magazine, and in particular the drumstick—it almost snapped! Suzanne and her friend barely made it past the entrance.

Original pictures sold at $50, copies at $25, and the drumstick a solid $100!

Within 30 minutes a security guard tapped her on the shoulder, enquiring, *'Excuse me, Ma'am, do you have a licence to sell on these premises?'*

She looked up with her young, sweet eyes and demurred. The security guard kindly escorted the pair off the premises. Suzanne and her friend scurried along together, counted the cash and couldn't believe what they had achieved: $800 dollars in 30 minutes at the age of 15! They blew it all at the mall, their parents dubious when their designer-clad daughters walked through the front door.

Suzanne is the type of person who, even at a young age, said they knew they were meant to be a salesperson when they grew up. These people are rare, but they do exist. To prepare herself for the world of work, she knew that going to university and majoring in commerce would help her to get ahead and be noticed by the best employers. She attended McMaster University in Hamilton, Ontario.

Near graduation, it was time to look for a job. Suzanne often read *Selling Power* magazine, which was very popular in North America and Canada. She'd always paid attention to the best companies to work for and Xerox continuously topped that list. She decided that this was where she'd begin her career. Seven intense interviews later, she landed the role, and driving to the office on her first day, she'd never been more excited about anything in life. Not even the day at the radio station when she met Soundgarden compared.

Xerox's primary business was selling large printers to big companies. Suzanne stepped into a junior sales role in the engineering vertical, which was one of the best introductions she could have received. Immediately she entered into intense training. Xerox had been pioneers in training salespeople to sell effectively, so it was no wonder that they continually topped the list of best companies to work for in the sales profession. Besides rigorous training, her exceptional mentors wanted her to succeed. That said, this wasn't an environment for everyone. You had to be ready for the intensity, and there is a reason it took seven interviews to secure a role there.

She remembers that every Monday they had a challenge, named Cold Call Mondays. The entire sales team blocked out the morning and together they blitzed the market. The sales floor roared; meetings were locked in, phones slammed down in anger, cheers of success and more. Sometimes the spotlight would shine on an individual. In a meeting room, one salesperson at a time would make a call on speaker, and the entire team would eagerly watch. If the phone slammed down because of an unsuccessful cold call, the salesperson would be heckled by the floor, but if they booked the meeting, the sales floor roared in applause.

This sales mentality even went outside of the office. Sometimes when Suzanne couldn't get hold of a key prospect on the phone, she'd show up at their offices unannounced and request to meet with the Chief Information Officer (CIO) there and then. In the rare cases they showed up, she even remembers her line:

> *'Did you know that engineering businesses spend 3% of their revenue on print and marketing costs? If you could reduce that by 25% what impact would that have on your bottom line?'*

The goal was to gain executive sponsorship to do a study on their printing and photocopier fleet as a basis for a proposal.

Suzanne assures me she sometimes landed the meeting with this ballsy approach!

Xerox shaped her, taught her what it took to be successful in sales, gave her constant exposure and world-class training. By year two she was rubbing shoulders with the Elite and she enjoyed five years of success at this company.

As the world moved on, the hardware became less and less interesting, because the focus was moving to software. Suzanne decided that she needed to get into big-ticket enterprise software deals. This was how she would move her career forward.

At the time, hospitals around the country were digitising their health records that had previously largely been paper-based. 3M was a big player in this market and had achieved record growth. Despite having relatively little knowledge about the market, Suzanne's fast success impressed 3M and they admired her ambition. They welcomed her to the team and she accepted.

3M as a company had achieved remarkable success in other areas of their diversified business, but in the Health Information Systems space, the division had underperformed several quarters in a row since its acquisition. There was one product in particular they hadn't managed to sell in four years! In Suzanne's first few weeks, a lead came through at a conference where she was 'manning' the 3M booth for this particular product. A tiny hospital, which was a 22-hour drive north of Toronto in a tiny town she'd never heard of. She qualified the lead on a call and discovered that their requirement was a perfect match for this product. Despite being a tiny hospital, the value for them would be huge.

Six months into her role at 3M, Suzanne secured this little hospital as a client, which turned out to be a major seven-figure deal. Her team, all much more experienced in sales, hadn't been able to achieve this level of success in four years.

The deal was complex and no big deal is ever a one-person performance; she received endless support from the solution engineers and senior leaders in the business. Together they won the deal. She admits that sometimes in sales it's about the right patch at the right time and this was definitely one of those situations. Yet it had been no accident that she worked for 3M at a time when the healthcare industry was going through rapid digitisation and that she had the sales skills to navigate a complex sale.

Whilst at university, Suzanne had spent a year in Singapore on an exchange programme and, since graduation, she'd been hard at work. Suzanne longed for an adventure. She took a brave decision and handed in her notice; with no job lined up, she packed her bags and moved to London. Just like that.

In London she knew that she'd find a new role, but decided she would take her time. Throughout her career she'd seen and heard many stories of companies that had taken off like rocket ships and the salespeople in for the ride advanced their careers at a much faster pace. She explored many industries and companies, and LinkedIn was one of them. This was 2013 and LinkedIn, although widely used, was still in its infancy.

The primary product that the LinkedIn sales team were selling took the form of premium subscriptions to professionals in recruitment or sales.

At LinkedIn the culture was unique: it was young, dynamic, and the company cared about your career growth. People were there to do something big. As Suzanne closed in on an offer from them, she also had an offer from a more established and well-known enterprise software company, with a bigger package. Sold on LinkedIn's culture, she accepted lower pay and joined the team. When I say lower pay, it was still significant and the OTE above six figures.

Although her move to LinkedIn was exciting, it was a tough move. It was one thing to learn a new product, but she also had the challenge of relearning how to write and talk using 'British' English, selling to multiple different departments and negotiating the budget from HR. To make matters more interesting, Suzanne's role was to launch LinkedIn in Africa.

As you can probably imagine, she has some fun stories from that time. Escorts of armed guards became the norm, but witnessing monkeys climb onto the LinkedIn sign at large social media events in the major cities, such as Lagos or Cape Town, never lost its sparkle. Suzanne had to learn how to ignore these distractions while presenting on stage to hundreds of spectators.

There was one story in particular that genuinely had her concerned for her safety. Upon landing at the airport in Lagos, Nigeria, where she was due to speak at Lagos Social Media week, she met with one of the region's business partners, and they headed to their cars. As is normal for business trips in the region, their armed guards followed. As they headed down dirt roads, the guards disappeared and their driver pulled over. Suddenly, out of the dark, faces appeared and headed towards the car.

BAM BAM, BAM... BAM BAM BAM...

Terrified, Suzanne frantically tried to figure out what was happening. All she could hear was African dialect being shouted back and forth. Unable to understand what they were saying, she felt tensions increase. The attackers had clamped the car and were demanding a ransom payment. Had their guards set them up?

Moments before they lost all hope, their armed guards came screeching around the corner and jumped out of their vehicle in militia gear, AK-47s cocked, and aggressively pointing their weapons at the attackers. Again, all Suzanne could hear was African dialect shouted back and forth, this time with a little more certainty. The guards banged on the car and demanded the attackers remove the clamps. Before they could fire any shots, the attackers removed the clamps and sprinted off into the night. Fortunately, everyone was unharmed. Next time, she feared they might not be so lucky.

DAMN!! What a welcome to the country!

Suzanne has many tales to tell of her adventures in Africa. Aside from this, she crushed her sales targets year on year. She always sought a bigger challenge and one day that challenge came along. She scoped out a major deal and forecast that it would be the largest ever new business deal in LinkedIn's history. Forced out of her comfort zone, she sought guidance and engaged the right support internally. Whilst assembling that team, she considered individual's skillsets and dynamic for this client. Determined that together they would win this deal!

Deals of this size can easily take over two years to close. Yet the client was ready. They wanted to get this done and had the motivation to drive it forward. Conversations started in March and, after intense negotiations, Suzanne and her media account manager alone closed a multi-million-dollar deal before the calendar year end. This was the largest new business deal in LinkedIn's history, for many years to come. That year Suzanne won the global sales award.

After seven years at LinkedIn, Suzanne has in fact won a global award twice, been to Presidents Club almost every year and mentored countless fellow salespeople to success.

Suzanne McGettigan's sales career wisdom

1. To be successful in sales, your mentality has a huge role to play, set your goals and do what it takes to achieve them.

2. Copy what works for the most successful salespeople, then make it your own as you build confidence and knowledge.

3. Always try new approaches. Always be open to learning and other perspectives.

UNWAVERING FOCUS

Phil, Hugh and Suzanne all have very different career stories and they have reached their levels of success in their own ways. Yet a constant between them is their focus on navigating their career forward and the results show. This behaviour is evident in all the stories shared throughout this book. Building a career plan can be a challenge, but who said it should be easy?

There are a few key principles to think about and we have gradually built on them throughout the book.

A very simple formula that you can base your career plan around is as follows:

1. Answer the following questions:

    1.1 Ultimately, where is it you'd like to reach in your career?

    1.2 What does the path look like to reach this destination?

    1.3 Where are you today on this journey?

2. Make a plan of how you will move forward.

The focus of this book is on your career, yet you can ask these same questions for your life overall. It works for friends, family, life partner, fitness, travel, charity, or whatever else is important to you.

Let's dig a little deeper into these questions from a career perspective.

1.1 Ultimately, where is it you'd like to reach in your career?

Fast forward to the end of your career: if you were in that moment and you reflected on your career, what is it you'd be proud to have achieved?

Perhaps it is that you would have reached the very top of the sales ranks and became a Chief Revenue Officer of a large, global public-listed enterprise software company and became very wealthy?

Maybe it was that you would have started your own business and achieved your vision to bring whatever it is you visualised to the world? The business could be small or big, focussed on making big money, or championing a noble cause. Entrepreneurship wears many hats.

Or perhaps you'd be proud to say you achieved a high level of work–life balance, led countless large transformational deals and invested your commission wisely? Rather than adding the immense amounts of pressure that comes with leadership roles, perhaps you decided to better spend your time with your loved ones and do what makes you happy deep down?

Really think about this and be clear on where you are heading.

1.2. What does the path look like to reach this destination?

People's paths to achieving big goals will naturally take all shapes and forms, as they should, because this isn't about someone else's journey—this is your journey.

Let's take an example. The end goal is to become a senior sales leader of a large enterprise software company in charge of their large global sales team. An admirable goal!

To break it down, there are several things you must show in your track record. That:

- you are a proven enterprise salesperson
- you are a proven sales leader of a team of people
- you are a proven leader of leaders
- you can lead a sales organisation to consistent growth

No doubt there are more things to add to that list, but for this exercise let's keep it simple. Again, if this is your goal, speak with people who have achieved it. Get their breakdown of how they reached that point in their careers. When you know what it is that you must do to get to a certain point in your career, you can plot a path of how you will achieve those milestones.

1.3. Where are you today on this journey?

The path ahead will look daunting and it should. This is your long-term goal. Today you might be an SMB software salesperson who is doing well, with a goal to become an Elite salesperson.

Maybe you are at the start of your sales career as a BDR and seek to gain the confidence to run a deal from start to close.

Or perhaps you are already selling enterprise software, yet you feel you could perform better. Your goal is to sharpen up and become one of the best at what you do.

Whatever it is, this is your starting point. Be honest with yourself; if you can't do that, then who can you be honest with? Don't forget to look back on what you've already achieved, and be proud of those achievements.

2. Make a plan of how you will move forward.

Now break it down. So far in this book you've learnt all that you need to have in your career plan to become an Elite salesperson. You know what to do to be in the heart of the action, to be an expert in your space, to be a student of sales, and now the master of your destiny.

At the start of this chapter, the software sales career path has been shared and also some things to be aware of. Use this knowledge to form your personal career plan for how you will achieve your career goals.

One thing to remember, which you may have already learnt on your journey, is that 'life happens'. Sometimes things are completely out of our control, such as storms that knock us off course, or suddenly catching a gigantic wave that accelerates our trajectory. Life is unpredictable.

As important as it is to have a solid plan for your career, allow some flexibility. For long-term goals, sometimes it is unwise to overthink them.

Once you've made your plan and you've made steady progress, be aware of your environment. Take notice of opportunities that appear, take notice of things that will knock you off course, and be ready to respond. If you respond, make sure that path continues to lead you in the direction you have set.

I'll end this chapter with a famous quotation by Stephen Covey, author of '*The 7 Habits of highly effective people*', who says:

'*Start with the end in mind.*'

CHAPTER 7

SEEK MENTORSHIP

Iron sharpens iron, and one man sharpens another.

PROVERBS 27:17

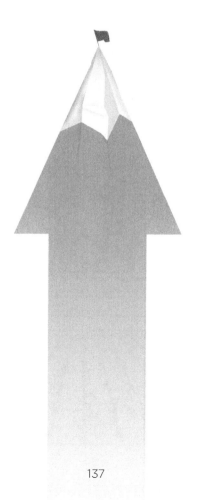

Mentorship is probably one of the most commonly used words in personal development, but also one of the least understood. What does it actually mean?

The Cambridge English Dictionary defines mentoring as the activity of giving a younger or less-experienced person help and advice over a period of time, especially at work or school.[1] Leaders constantly encourage aspiring employees to seek a mentor and develop their skillset, but this can leave people more lost than focussed. A commonly held belief is that a mentor should guide you in all areas, that they should be your 'career mentor' or/and 'life mentor'. Which in theory sounds fantastic!

In reality, that's a tough thing to achieve from one person and you soon realise that mentorship comes in many forms. For example, there is a lengthy list of skills required to become a successful salesperson:

- Cold calling
- Presenting
- Negotiation
- Proposal building
- Developing business cases
- Account planning
- Territory planning

The list goes on…

To find a mentor who can help you learn the entire skillset would require an enormous commitment from them, so it's a big ask. Some people are lucky enough to find mentors to help with such broad development, but it's rare.

More commonly you realise that mentorship could be as minor as providing guidance on just one thing, such as cold calling or proposal building. The mentor will give you their perspective based on their own experience. When you ask multiple people, you develop a broader perspective, because there really is not one size that fits all.

Take Marcus in Chapter 5, for example. When he joined Finsda he became the best of a group of six or seven people, and he did so by learning from them all.

Mentorship is the act of providing advice to someone less experienced than you, whether that be about big or small things. If you develop a long-term relationship with this mentor, fantastic, but that is not what defines being mentored.

Mentoring is important in all areas of life, and has been evident in all the stories shared so far. When I asked Elite salespeople what three things they'd recommend to an aspirational Elite salesperson, mentorship was the second most common answer. So why is it the last pillar if it is the second most common answer?

The reason is that mentorship is present in all the pillars. Here is why:

1. When you are trying to identify how to place yourself in the heart of the action, you will find that one of the most effective ways to do that is to speak with someone who is already there. This person's experience will give you a more in-depth perspective in comparison with online research. If you then speak with multiple people who are in the heart of the action, it will broaden your perspective further.

2. Once you've identified the heart of the action, your next focus should be to become an expert in that space. Within your organisation you're likely to meet many people with deep knowledge of your industry and products. Picking their brains will speed up your development and allow you to form your own perspective.

3. Nothing beats experience for developing your sales skills. To learn different sales methodologies, reading self-development books and listening to podcasts will broaden your knowledge. But people are

not clones. If you speak with multiple successful people about their sales approach, it will give you a fresh perspective on how to approach sales in a way that works for you, by leveraging their experience. The sooner we learn, the sooner we achieve our own success.

4. Finally, for taking control of your career direction, mentorship is one of the most important aspects. When we look ahead to where we want to go, we don't just look at titles; we look at the people, and specifically, the people who have achieved what we want to achieve. They inspire us to do what it takes to get there so we can feel that sense of achievement. Navigating this path is highly complex and in sales careers there is rarely a straight line. Speaking with people who have already achieved what we want to achieve, and understanding how they did it, is the most effective way to build a solid career plan that works.

Those who place finding a mentor as one of the most important pillars in building their careers often move forward faster than those who rely on their own intuition.

There are several stories that stood out for mentorship from the research project and you'll see the impact it has had on their careers.

Jefferson Mangus

The friendliness of Jefferson Mangus' voice rings through as he speaks, which pinpoints him back to his small hometown just outside Oklahoma City, Oklahoma. From a young age he had a sense of adventure and was always outdoors playing with his friends. Whilst at university, he spent a year of study in Denmark at the Aarhus School of Business, which exposed him to an entirely different culture.

During this adventure in Aarhus he met his future wife, Juliette, who was from France. Upon graduation, they both went back to their respective countries to save money, in order to someday be together. Though Juliette thought cowboys and Oklahoma football were great, she felt together they might prefer the vibrant New York City.

As a new graduate, Jefferson's bank account was in the red, so he needed to make some cash to pay for a deposit to rent an apartment in New York City, and also have enough to eat whilst starting a new job. Where he grew up, there were commonly heavy hailstorms and tornadoes annually, with hailstones the size of golf balls. This caused havoc to people's businesses and properties, in particular their roofs.

A local roofing company's sales strategy was to go door to door to sell their repair service for damaged roofs on the back of insurance claims. They claimed that their top salespeople, with no previous sales experience, earned over $100,000 a year. Jefferson eagerly joined the team!

He and the sales team literally chased storms around the state. They entered towns when it was safe and knocked on every door before competitors muscled in. Door-to-door sales is a tough business, particularly in rural areas. Many times Jefferson recalls entering a property to be greeted with the barrel of a shotgun. It's safe to say, they fired no shots!

After several months barely selling any roofs, with the little money he made being taxed heavily, he realised they had sold him a lie! Fortunately, he had just about scraped together enough money to start his new life in New York with his girlfriend.

New York didn't quite provide the warm welcome they had dreamed of. Not only were apartments more expensive than they expected, but demand was so high that it was difficult to secure one. To make matters worse, most landlords demanded they earned twice the monthly rent in salary. As both he and his girlfriend were at the start of their careers, they made little money.

Luckily a family who had a spare room took them in. They happily stayed there for six years.

With almost no work experience, Jefferson had few career options. He secured a job for a uniform company selling to auto body shops. Often he would find himself selling uniforms to tough audiences in the rough neighbourhoods of Brooklyn. On multiple occasions the police pulled him over, day or night, puzzled why he was in these rough parts of town. They recommended he left immediately, for his own safety.

Eventually, he sought a safer working environment. Next up, he landed a job selling coffee machines and supplies in the the office buildings of Manhattan. Finally, he felt like he was making it. He shadowed the established salespeople and, after getting the hang of it, he made some decent money. Ambition kicked in, however, and he realised there could be no progression in this company. People had been in their positions for years and to get promoted, you'd have to wait for someone to be fired, leave or, to put it bluntly, die.

For good reason he therefore explored other career opportunities and discovered the recruitment industry, which is a career with no barriers to success and which actively seeks people like Jefferson. Several recruitment firms offered him an interview and he landed a role at Michael Page. Now he wasn't just having meetings in the Manhattan buildings, he actually worked in one—and of all places, the famous Chrysler Building.

That said, success wasn't instant for Jefferson at Michael Page. As a dyslexic, he often finds he takes a little longer than most to learn new skills. Yet when he takes something on board, he's never afraid to stand up and tell the world! Michael Page has a culture resembling a family, so many colleagues spent time with Jefferson to help him learn the role. Recruitment became his life and eventually he started to place candidates. He was proud to improve people's lives by helping them progress their careers.

Jefferson made a name for himself, such that his colleagues started to turn to him for advice, and his confidence grew. A story he'll never forget is when he landed a client with ambitions to rapidly expand their business. They tasked Jefferson with building a new team. Committed to the task, he focussed entirely on this client and formed a solid team, all ready to start. The deal was worth $100,000 to Michael Page, over six times larger than the average $15,000. It had taken him a couple of quarters to build this team and his colleagues at Michael Page were excited to see him pull it off.

At the last minute, disaster struck. The client pulled the plug. They decided that it would cost too much for them to hire an entire team with Michael Page, despite all the work Jefferson and they had already done.

Devastated and unable to cover his shortage, the loss hit Jefferson hard. That was one of the worst quarters in Jefferson's sales career. However, being resilient, he quickly dusted himself off with the support of his colleagues and learnt a valuable lesson to never put all your eggs in one basket. Soon he was back on track. Top people never stay down for long.

At the time, LinkedIn was on the rise and Jefferson used the platform daily to find new candidates for live job roles. LinkedIn made his life significantly easier! He was not alone. Almost all recruitment professionals found value from the platform, so much so that several of his colleagues joined LinkedIn's sales team. They advised Jefferson to make the move and, after taking some time to assess if it was the right opportunity for him, he applied and secured an interview.

Although Jefferson had proved himself in sales, the bar to joining LinkedIn was exceptionally high. Industry highfliers were eagerly interviewing there to join the sales team, not just from recruitment, but software sales too. Jefferson rose to the challenge and made a solid case of why they should hire him.

LinkedIn sought salespeople who had a solid track record, but with plenty of room for growth. They saw enormous potential in Jefferson and offered him the role. Without a second thought, he accepted. Finally, this was his opportunity to become an Elite salesperson! Not only that, but his new place of work would be in the Empire State Building, a location he could only have dreamed of years before.

The induction process at LinkedIn informs new recruits that their career trajectory is about to change. Those who join this company experience fast-paced professional and personal growth, and even when they one day leave the company, that trajectory continues. This is a company that invests in its people.[2]

Jefferson's role was to sell LinkedIn recruitment solutions to recruitment companies, an industry he knew well. But there was a serious amount to learn in terms of the tech, the digital industry and enterprise sales, so he had to adapt fast.

More motivated than he had ever been, he committed to success. First, Jefferson identified the top performers at LinkedIn, picked their brains about what had worked for them and listened to their calls. Next, he reviewed his performance and had endless one-to-one meetings with his manager. Many advised him to read sales books, yet his dyslexia made that difficult. Instead, he turned to podcasts and audiobooks.

This support and focus helped him to develop into the professional that he needed to be. Deal after deal he edged closer to his sales targets, before finally experiencing breakaway success. Every year Jefferson was one of the top 10% of the company's salespeople and attended the President's Club. He had joined the Elite in sales.

The lessons he has learnt became habits. One of the most effective methods he found was to have strategy sessions with his colleagues who were top performers; those meetings often went like this:

1. Jefferson would present the opportunity to his colleagues and give some background on the company in question.

2. Together they would assess what pain points this company was experiencing.

3. With this knowledge they could then map out the right solution and how to add maximum value.

4. Finally, they'd create a sales strategy to ensure all the right stakeholders were involved, no red flags were missed and how to create a solid business case.

As, or if, the deal progressed, quite often they'd reassess the opportunity to realign the sales strategy if necessary; sales requires nimble operators.

Most people don't ask for help, yet for Jefferson it has always been second nature and as he always takes others' advice on board, people love to help him and see him succeed. It works both ways. Many people have asked Jefferson for advice on their deals and, without thinking twice, he comes to their aid.

LinkedIn isn't just about financial success; they are big believers in philanthropy and support their employees with their own causes. For example, Haiti has long suffered natural disasters such as earthquakes and tropical storms. In 2016, the destructive Hurricane Matthew hit the country, killing at least 580 people and leaving 35,000 homeless.[3] The news struck Americans to the core and it inspired Jefferson to come to the country's aid.

Immediately he researched what he could do and learnt that charities sought people to raise money to build schools, and people to help build them. To help, he would need to raise at least $30,000 and pull together a team of 6 people. In 5 days he raised $60,000, double the target, and amassed a team of 15 initially, though 8 or 9 did not see it through to the end. They built one hell of a school!

The following year he raised $100,000, with 25 people for a project in Senegal. The year after that, with a team of 50 people, he collected $200,000, building 3 schools in Nepal. He'd started something bigger than himself and was immensely proud. Life at LinkedIn was good!

Some years later, a company called Gong secured a deal with LinkedIn. Gong provides a solution that analyses salespeople's calls to identify the traits of both top performers and underperformers. Advanced NLP (Natural Language Processing) and ML (Machine Learning) algorithms power their platform. These insights show salespeople exactly how to shape themselves into top performers. As Jefferson was a top performer at LinkedIn, his calls were used to help train the platform.

Jefferson's mind was blown and so he instantly championed Gong.

Despite all that he had achieved at LinkedIn and his love for the company, he had reached a point where he no longer felt challenged. Year on year he was consistently one of the top 10% in the sales department. There was room to grow into management, but Jefferson didn't want to take that path.

Gong's growth was fierce and Jefferson enquired about a senior enterprise sales role. Here was a product and company he believed could challenge him. Unfortunately, they had no vacancies at that point, but told him that they would love him to join the team when they did.

Six months later they got back in touch and, after a short interview round, offered Jefferson the role with a fantastic package, which he instantly accepted. To make things even more exciting, shortly after he started, they secured investment worth $65m to scale the business. No doubt Jefferson is strapped in for a rocket-ship journey!

Along his path, like all Elite salespeople, Jefferson built the pillars of his career over time. The pillar that has had the biggest impact on his career is mentorship. His dyslexia forced him to seek help from others and work closely with them to learn. Little did he know at the time that this is the most effective form of personal development.

Jefferson did not just take the advice of his mentors, but also implemented it and did them proud. This is the personal reward mentors receive. It's no wonder that when Jefferson learnt about Gong, a product built on mentorship, it immediately resonated with him.

Jefferson Mangus's sales career wisdom

1. Build your network both in person and on LinkedIn.

2. Identify top salespeople, try to meet them and learn as much as you can from them.

3. Read the sales books, listen to the podcasts and develop your skillset.

A commonality of those who place large importance on mentorship is that they move faster forward in their career than others. Some of us dreamt of acceleration from as young as we can remember.

Ryan Chapman

Imagine piloting a fighter jet, the fastest and most deadly aircraft found in the sky. Some are capable of speeds faster than 2,000mph and possess weapon systems that can inflict mass destruction.[4] Ryan Chapman, from a young age, dreamt of being a fighter pilot.

Ryan grew up in Papua New Guinea and it exposed him to a world many of us only see on the news. Poverty, crime and suffering surrounded him. His parents moved the family back to their country of origin, New Zealand, to provide a better future. During his education, Ryan became very fond of rugby; not just fond, but also very talented. His coaches all believed he had the potential to make a career in the sport.

Performing at a high level and playing for some of the best teams, Ryan made a name for himself. Yet his dream of becoming a pilot never left him. He started flying at age 14, and at 18 he moved to Sydney to enrol at the Sydney Aerobatic School to learn how to be an aerobatic pilot, dropping rugby at around this time. As much as he loved rugby, his passion was always to be a pilot.

Barrel-rolling and somersaulting small planes through the air, Ryan got into aerial aerobatics, with the support from his wife. Ryan won his first contest in 2007. After competing in Australia and then New Zealand, Ryan and his wife, Ivana, made the move to Toronto, Canada in 2011 to start a new life.

Like most students, to make ends meet he needed a part-time job, which led him to sales. A company called WBR (Worldwide Business Research) held conferences on a variety of topics in e-commerce and finance. Ryan's job was to cold call senior executives and have them buy a ticket, sponsor the event and/or come to the show. It was very much an entry-level role. Staff attrition was high, as many struggled to find their feet. Ryan found a mentor who helped him learn the ropes and eventually he delivered his sales targets. During this time, Ryan was progressing towards a career in aviation. But his mentor showed him the world of sales and how to be successful.

His success did not go unnoticed, and WBR promoted him to a sales manager of five other people. Ryan ran sales campaigns for the conferences and seminars, while training and motivating his team. Soon he realised he was good at sales, a path he hadn't even considered as a career. In sales he could make great money, be home every night and fly planes as a hobby.

For the first time, despite being passionate about being a pilot, the realisation of his long-term dream as a career hit him hard. He would constantly be on the move, from country to country, with little time for rest and to devote to his friends and family. Any decent money came later in the career and Ryan seriously questioned whether being a pilot was the right path.

Ryan eventually decided that he would not fly planes for a living, but that flying would remain a hobby. The thing he loved most was the thrill of aerobatics, which is absolutely not something commercial airlines can endorse with hundreds of passengers onboard. Imagine that! The issue with this is that piloting planes is an expensive hobby. Fortunately, the career path he chose pays exceptionally well, if you perform. His time at WBR had inspired him and Ryan decided that the right career for him would be in sales.

In 2012, Ryan spoke to his mentor from WBR to pick his brains on how best to move his sales career forward. At this time, Ryan had an opportunity at ExactTarget, the No. 1 cross-channel marketing platform at the time. Ryan knew nothing about digital marketing, but his mentor gave him some encouragement and told him to do it.

ExactTarget had developed an industry-leading cross-channel digital marketing solution to address a big problem that marketers faced, namely marketing automation.

Ryan was slightly nervous as he had zero knowledge on the subject, but his mentor convinced him that, if he could fly a plane, he could learn a marketing automation tool and how to sell it.

His impressive successes in other areas of his life, early signs of success in sales, and a dedicated work ethic impressed the leaders at ExactTarget. They offered him a role. Cheekily, he pushed for a role in enterprise sales, as this is where the big money is. But they laughed and said, prove yourself in the small-to-medium segment first, and then we can talk. With great excitement, he accepted ExactTarget's offer and started his career in technology sales.

Day one at the new job overwhelmed him. He knew even less than he had thought, and he thought he knew nothing! Ryan made a 30, 60 and 90 day plan. First, he'd dedicate himself to learning the product, then he'd build his pipeline and after that he'd secure his first deals. ExactTarget had a structured on-boarding process; however, Canada was a new market. Ryan's first goal was to get to know everyone in the business and he arranged one-to-one's with the entire team, including the CEO, Scott Dorsey.

This process taught him a lot about the industry, the product, client success and effective selling. In addition, many of his colleagues offered their ongoing support. This solid network gave him the confidence that he would make a success of his role.

Six months later, Ryan was selling to enterprise. ExactTarget had kept their word, as Ryan had kept his.

Enterprise is the starting line of becoming Elite and Ryan knew this. Fortunately, he was surrounded by exceptional salespeople and they took him under their wing. Everyone wanted to see this young man succeed.

He recalls the moment at which he felt he'd truly made it, when he received a $120,000 commission payment. He'd closed two large deals and several smaller ones. Through determination, continuous education and mentorship, he'd rapidly become an Elite salesperson.

In sales, Ryan believes that you create your own jackpot. You decide how much you want to earn and put in place a plan to achieve that goal. With the right focus and determination, the results will come, but you need to be patient and thoughtful in your approach.

With stellar sales performances across the team, ExactTarget flourished and the client base surpassed 4,500. In March 2012, they successfully filed for an IPO, which made many people a lot of money.[5] ExactTarget was a leader in the space, and its key rivals included Neolane and Responsys.

As the marketing automation market matured, it caught the attention of technology titans such as Oracle, Adobe and Salesforce. So much so, it ignited a race between them to build the most sophisticated marketing cloud, which is a combination of digital marketing solutions. An acquisition frenzy began as none of the titans had marketing technology (martech) of their own.

2013 turned out to be one of the most defining years in this acquisition frenzy. That June, Salesforce acquired ExactTarget for $2.5bn, the same month Adobe acquired Neolane for $600m.[6,7] Oracle were a little later to the acquisition party when they acquired Responsys in December 2013 for $1.5bn.[8]

The competitive landscape stepped up to a whole new level. The way they sold martech went through a transformation, just as the marketing industry itself had.

For ExactTarget, Salesforce acted as a huge and powerful sales machine. Now they would have inroads into almost every major account on their target list. New business sales turned into cross-selling, which made life a lot easier for the sales team. It was by no means a walk in the park, but it is possible to achieve a lot more in the sales year when you represent a brand like Salesforce.

The situation thrilled many on the team; it gave them an opportunity to grow and develop their career faster than before. Yet there were many who couldn't get along with big corporate culture. They missed the wild west days of an explosive start-up. Ryan was part of that group, and eventually, after much soul-searching, he left.

After the acquisition and excellent run Ryan had had at ExactTarget, financially he could take his time in his next move. As he had built in-depth knowledge in digital marketing, he advised start-ups on their sales and marketing strategies. Most notable of these was a business called Sailthru, which was like ExactTarget, yet nowhere near the scale. He acted for them as an interim sales director, helping them penetrate the enterprise sales segment. Ryan learned a lot during his time at Sailthru, and as with ExactTarget, was grateful for the experience.

This was a grand time in his life where he could spend more time with his Ivana, his wife and their newborn son, still pilot planes regularly and help other businesses grow, before his next big career move. Ryan looks at companies as investments; if he joins one, they need to have the potential to be the No. 1 player. Key things he examines include:

- the leadership team
- their growth potential and customer base
- whether he can develop professionally at that company

A company called Sprinklr caught his attention. They had developed an enterprise-grade social media management tool and had become the leader in the industry. Sprinklr was on the cusp of developing a new category called CXM (Customer Experience Management). Large enterprises across the globe had adopted their solution and the company was experiencing rapid growth. In March 2015, they raised $46m to fund their expansion, which pushed their valuation past $1bn.[9]

By mid-2016, Sprinklr had high expectations for Canada, which convinced Ryan that Sprinklr would be an excellent investment of his time. He joined the team as an enterprise account executive with the single goal of making Sprinklr the No. 1 CXM player in Canada.

Even though he had deep knowledge of digital marketing and a solid base of enterprise sales experience, he met many salespeople more successful than him. As with ExactTarget, Ryan met with the top performers and senior people to learn all he could. However, unlike ExactTarget, this time he was a little more selective about whom he spent his time with. With a dedicated focus on learning the product inside out, stepping up his knowledge and building his pipeline, Ryan chipped away at his number. He ramped up quickly and soon delivered his sales targets.

Three years into his tenure at Sprinklr, Ryan had become one of the top performers in the company. They rewarded him with a promotion to become a Global Strategic Account Executive, which is the very top of the individual contributor career path. He couldn't have been happier!

Ryan Chapman's sales career wisdom

1. Beware of the buzz, tech companies are usually very good at sales and marketing; sieve through the noise and see the facts. The ones that stand up are the ones that you should invest your time in, ignore the rest.

2. As you progress your career remain humble, there's always something new you can learn and the moment you think you know it all is the moment you'll fall behind.

3. Down this path there will be times you feel you're failing, don't go at it alone, meet and talk with people who have been successful and learn all you can from them. Mentorship is the number one thing in personal development.

Most of the time we must go out and seek our first mentors, yet for some of us, we find them in our own homes.

Madeleine Storr

'Combination Cambination' was Madeleine Storr's first sales venture when she was a young girl. Her older and younger sister were equal partners in the business. The kitchen dining room became the office in their family home, which was just outside of London in the county of Surrey. It's a county famed for its stunning scenery.

The Storr girls would go around the family home, find items of interest and attempt to sell them back to their parents. Fierce negotiations took place, just as their mother had taught them. The Storrs' mother ran a car sales business and their father worked in politics.

Maybe Madeleine was destined to be a salesperson?

During school breaks, she would help with the family business, whether that meant customer service, accounts, or her favourite activity, selling cars. Her mother one day hoped that her daughters would take over the business.

Madeleine was never that excited about university, but all her friends were going and she didn't want to miss out. She went with the flow and was accepted to study law. Within two days she left. Instead, for the next year she worked full-time in a pub and the family car business.

Throughout the year, her friend's stories from university made her envious. She decided that she had to pull herself together, take a little longer to think about what she would study and go with a purpose. Madeleine settled on a degree in business with French and German, mainly because she would get to spend a year abroad.

Despite having little enthusiasm for study, she now admits that it really helped to round her knowledge. The year abroad was particularly memorable, split between Munich where she worked in recruitment, and Paris where she worked for a *New York Times* syndicate selling videos and photos to other publications. She found recruitment to be very aggressive! Luckily for her, all those years in car sales really showed. Quickly she achieved success and lived a luxury lifestyle compared to her student friends. But she saved most of her commission.

The last year at university was tough. She missed the buzz of sales. Yet she persevered and graduated with a solid grade. Fortunately, she hadn't spent all her commission and so was able to afford a few nice holidays without having to work part-time. This made the year more bearable.

Madeleine's first job upon graduation was at a start-up accelerator where she pitched ideas to investors for seed investment. A memorable moment was when she pitched to Doug Richard, a famous American entrepreneur and investor who starred in a popular BBC programme *Dragons' Den*. The commercials of the deal were weak, so he tore them to pieces. It was a very uncomfortable encounter! Yet it taught her a lesson she'd never forget, which was always to be prepared.

Before long she concentrated on how she would develop her career. The rise of digital marketing had caught her attention and she focussed there. Madeleine thought that there would be no better way to learn about it than to become a marketing manager, so she applied to several companies.

Kind Consumer took her on as their marketing manager. This company develops small inhalation and nicotine-vaping devices. They gave her full rein of marketing such as the website, advertising, PR, packaging and events. She spent a couple of years in this role, gaining hands-on experience as a marketer responsible for growing a brand.

As Madeleine's knowledge of digital marketing grew, she realised that digital marketing tools are pivotal to the company's success. Kind Consumer used several of them, so rather than working for the company that used the tools, she thought it would be a better career move to be part of the company that developed the tools. She applied to join the customer-facing teams of several companies doing exactly that.

Her top priority was to join the best company she could and grow from there. Impressed by her initiative, she received an offer from an analytics company.

Before accepting, there was one last offer on the table that she wanted, which was from Salesforce. At that point they were seeking a customer success manager to look after the German and French client base, based in London in their marketing cloud division. At the time, Madeleine wasn't sure that she wanted to work for a large corporate, but the incredible buzz of the company sucked her in.

It was instantly clear that the interview process differed greatly from the others where she knew that she could have walked straight into roles. Salesforce challenged her and made her question whether she was ready for this role.

She had ten interviews in which they tested her skills in language, maths, client relationships, presentations and more. After putting her through her paces, Salesforce offered her the role. Here she knew that she could learn more than at any other company she had interviewed with. Madeleine eagerly accepted the role. Luckily she had studied French and German at university!

Within a month, Salesforce realised that Madeleine was better suited for an account management role and she was promoted to a role focussed on increasing client spend. The product she looked after was a social media advertising management tool and her client base was comprised mainly of agencies or large brands. The more the clients spent, the more Salesforce made.

Her experience to that point had prepared her for the role. Being able to speak the language helped to build trust with prospects and her time in sales helped with closing. Taking a consultative approach, she quickly became the top performer in the team.

The sales team were looking for a replacement for the German market, to secure new contracts with a new adtech tool that allowed Salesforce's clients to connect their CRM data to the social ad networks, for more effective targeting. Salesforce asked Madeleine to cover the patch in the interim until they found someone new, yet she spun it and asked whether, if she could prove herself, they would hire her for the role? Salesforce accepted.

Immediately she focussed on upskilling as this was an enormous step up. Fortunately, Salesforce employed some of the best salespeople in the industry and Madeleine had no fear of asking them for help. They continually advised her. She also shadowed several of her colleagues in meetings. Quickly, her skillset developed.

Salesforce paused the interview process for the German market and within a quarter saw that Madeleine was very much ready for this role. They offered her the position. She'd made it into enterprise tech sales.

To step up her personal development, Madeleine identified a high-performing female sales leader at Salesforce and asked for her to be her formal career coach. This person accepted and wasted no time in helping Madeleine focus on the right things. In addition, she took courses at the IAB (Internet Advertising Bureau) to learn digital advertising in depth, attended industry events every year, and took sales courses. A course she recalls that had a large impact on her skills was with Cambridge University, on negotiation. Lastly, for every deal she lost, she conducted a post-mortem to learn from her mistakes. With the right plan and foundations, it prepared her.

In year 1 she achieved 720% of her number; 267% in year 2, and 240% in year 3. Unsurprisingly, in year 4 she was promoted to sales manager. Every year Salesforce promoted her to sell more complex solutions, invited her to Presidents Club and awarded her with pay rises.

Madeleine had consistently become one of the top performers in her department and one of the highest paid in all the Salesforce EMEA sales team. Yet she remains humble and never stops learning.

Madeleine Storr's sales career wisdom

1. Be relentless in achieving your success, do what it takes to succeed.

2. Don't let failures on the path knock you back, pick yourself up and learn from them, it's part of the job.

3. Become the product expert in whatever you do, don't rely on others for your success, take ownership.

FINDING MENTORS

Whether you, like Madeleine, find a formal mentor who can help you in your overall career, or if you pick the brains of several people to form your own unique style, as Ryan did, or if you find people to coach you to success, like Jefferson, the act of asking others to help you with a specific thing is mentorship. Asking people for help can seem like a daunting task, especially if you ask people you don't know that well. Yet how we approach this has a major impact on the effectiveness of mentorship.

Picture yourself as the successful person you one day hope to become. Two people approach you to ask you to mentor them. One is a rising star, the type of person who strives to make their life better, values your achievements and listens to you. The second is someone who refuses to get into work early or stay late, who will not spend their free time on personal development and their only goal is to make more money.

Which person of the two would you mentor? Probably the first, right? But why?

The most frustrating thing for mentors is when they advise someone who then does nothing with that advice. Naturally it motivates people to see success come from their efforts, and even though mentorship is giving back, the same principles apply. When someone mentors you, they want to see you become successful, otherwise they wouldn't put in the time to help you. Give mentors the confidence that you are a person who will value their time, that will not only listen to their advice, but will also do something with it. As a mentee, it's our duty to make our mentors proud!

There's a reason mentorship is the last pillar rather than the first, because it applies to all the pillars.

With the knowledge provided in this book, you should be able to:

1. Identify the market you would like to focus on.

2. Make a plan of how you can become an expert.

3. Identify your strengths and weaknesses in sales and develop your own personal development plan.

4. Plot out your career plan to your desired destiny.

Yet even with your own research, there will still be gaps in that plan, things that have been a little difficult to figure out without in-depth research, and things you haven't even thought about yet. This is an area where mentors can add a lot of value. Remember, you can have multiple mentors; in fact, it's better to have several perspectives.

Before approaching mentors, you need to be clear on what help you require, to show them you will value their time. A simple process to gain a mentor is as follows:

1. Focus on the area or areas that you would like to improve and write it down.

2. Identify between three and five successful people in that area.

3. Connect with them, with a clear message.

4. Value their time, listen to them, and do something with that knowledge.

If you work for a decent company, then it's likely your colleagues will possess the knowledge you seek. Remember, it's in their shared interest to help you so that your organisation will succeed. Approach them with confidence.

If you're not in an organisation that you would like to grow in, or one that employs the right people to help you, or perhaps not currently in an organisation altogether, then you may require a more creative approach.

Here is an example of something that you could do:

1. Identify an organisation that has many Elite salespeople, the type of organisation that you'd like to work in.

2. Examine the profiles of the salespeople on LinkedIn and identify the Elite. Typically they will have been in individual contributor roles for eight or more years, having progressed through the ranks. Often they will share their achievements on their profile.

3. Connect with these people on LinkedIn, with a personalised message that acknowledges their success.

Besides the digital approach, you could also attend networking events for salespeople. When you are there, don't be shy and be clear on what you seek when you introduce yourself. Even if you already have access to exceptional people who can help you grow, there is no harm in this proactive approach. If you broaden the number of successful people in your network, it will broaden your development.

You can repeat this simple process on not just every pillar of your sales career, at any time, but also in practically all areas of life.

As you step through your career and master the skillset required to be an Elite salesperson, naturally you will need to seek new mentors more suited for the next wave of your personal development. Some mentors can stay with us for a long time; others for only minor parts of our journey. The important thing is that you keep developing and keep seeking people that you can learn from as you develop your skillset.

Mentorship should always be at the core of personal development.

CHAPTER 8

SIMULTANEOUSLY BUILD THE PILLARS

Something very special happens as you build the pillars simultaneously in your career; you will naturally stand out as an individual. You choose to specialise in an area because you are motivated to learn about it, the career path that you plot out leads you down a path towards achieving your own personal ambitions, you embrace the sales skills and methodologies that most naturally fit with your personality and the mentors you surround yourself with are all individuals in their own right, with their own wisdom to impart.

Throughout your sales career you'll hear many people advise you to be authentic. Never be a robot reading from a script. That can be a hard thing to understand how to do. Building the pillars in your career is a sure way to do it. How could you not be authentic when you have done so?

At the end of each interview in the research project, you'll have noticed that I was curious to learn what advice Elite salespeople give to those who seek to emulate them. Below you will find my summary of the results.

When you have read their answers, can you identify the commonalities?

CHAPTER 2: INTRODUCTION TO THE ELITE

Haig Hanessian

1. Work harder than anyone else.

2. Develop yourself and stick to the methodology.

3. Seek mentors.

Mandy Smithson

1. Be bold and just go for it. 'Fake it till you make it'.

2. Don't be afraid to fail and to learn from your mistakes.

3. Seek mentors and coaches that can help you develop.

Dan Czasnicki

1. Understand what makes people successful in your role or the role you seek, develop that skillset and prove you can be that person.

2. Structure and hard work are key to success. Be organised.

3. Prove you are a person who people can trust by acting as a professional at all times.

CHAPTER 3: PILLAR 1:
THE HEART OF THE ACTION

Joachim Haas

1. Go deep, immerse yourself and learn everything you can about your space.

2. Challenge yourself, don't be afraid to fail and, when you do, make sure you learn fast and get back up on your feet.

3. Most importantly, find a mentor. You'll need the guidance to progress.

Ben Tunstall

1. Be prepared to learn.

2. Throw yourself in at the deep end.

3. Put in the graft and, above all, commit yourself.

CHAPTER 4: PILLAR 2:
INDUSTRY EXPERT

Steve Mason

1. Find your passion as soon as possible. When you align your core values, it allows you to tap into your full potential and trigger a higher sales performance.

2. Once you find this thing go deep, you need to become an expert. Once you are an expert it will allow you to become a trusted advisor which is a cut above the rest.

3. With both things aligned, you then need people to buy into you and your vision. Develop your public speaking and presentation skills.

Ben Jaderstrom

1. Become an industry expert.

2. Surround yourself with successful people, learn what they do and how they do it.

3. Practice makes perfect. Start with small business sales to drive high volumes which allows you to refine and improve your sales skills before you progress on to enterprise sales.

Jon Levesque

1. Become an expert in what you do and commit to excellence.

2. Put time on the bike. You cannot escape the value of experience.

3. Never stop learning and accept change.

CHAPTER 5: PILLAR 3: STUDENT OF SALES

Marcus

1. Choose your mentors, shadow them and understand what it is they do to be successful.

2. Understand what success looks like, measure it and do whatever is required to stay on track.

3. Deeply understand your market and profession, commit to personal education.

Brendan McLaughlin

1. Beyond all, be yourself, time goes by quickly, love what you do and don't pretend to be something you are not.

2. Appreciate those who help you succeed, mentorship and help from others is the number one driving force for success.

3. Hone your craft and take training seriously.

Bonus

4. Persistence & tenacity will always help you develop your skills to be more effective.

Justin Golding

1. Be in the right place at the right time. A company that's growing fast, in a hot space, that momentum will propel you.

2. Focus on developing your skillset as a way of progressing your career, don't fall into the trap of going into management too soon, progress into more complex sales first.

3. Be true to who you are, don't let organisations shape you into a robot. Yet don't let your ego impede personal development, it's important that you grow.

CHAPTER 6: PILLAR 4: MASTER OF YOUR OWN DESTINY

Phil Nyborg

1. Earn your spot in meetings, become an expert in what you do and always focus on adding value to your client.

2. Always push yourself and aim high. Great things do not happen in your comfort zone.

3. Understand what makes you tick, dig deep, connect with your passion and use that to drive you forward, it will allow you to become authentic. Authenticity instantly builds trust with clients.

Hugh Darvall

1. Find a company you can be successful in and build on that success, stick it out and go as far as you can.

2. Personal development is key to getting ahead, take it seriously and learn the skills necessary to progress.

3. Sales is a rollercoaster of a career in which you will have your highs and lows. Don't let this affect you, it's important you have thick skin and remember to celebrate the good times.

Suzanne McGettigan

1. To be successful in sales, your mentality has a huge role to play, set your goals and do what it takes to achieve them.

2. Copy what works for the most successful salespeople, then make it your own as you build confidence and knowledge.

3. Always try new approaches, be open to learning and other people's perspectives.

CHAPTER 7: PILLAR 5: MENTORSHIP

Jefferson Mangus

1. Build your network both in person and on LinkedIn.

2. Identify top salespeople, try to meet them and learn as much as you can from them.

3. Read the sales books, listen to the podcasts and develop your skillset.

Ryan Chapman

1. Beware of the buzz, tech companies are usually very good at sales and marketing, sieve through the noise and see the facts. The ones that stand up are the ones that you should invest your time in, ignore the rest.

2. As you progress your career remain humble, there's always something new you can learn and the moment you think you know it all is the moment you'll fall behind.

3. Down this path there will be times you feel you're failing, don't go at it alone, meet and talk with people who have been successful and learn all you can from them. Mentorship is the number one thing in personal development.

Madeline Storr

1. Be relentless in achieving your success, do what it takes to succeed.

2. Don't let failures on the path knock you back, pick yourself up and learn from them, it's part of the job.

3. Become the product expert in whatever you do, don't rely on others for your success, take ownership.

As you can see, there is a broad range of answers, and some repeat the same points but express them differently. Keep in mind that these are only 17 of the 50 answers received. When I reviewed the answers to identify commonalities, I defined 9 categories.

THE 9 CATEGORIES AND DISCOVERIES

1. 65% said to focus on learning, such as sales process, product, industry etc.

2. 49% said mentorship.

3. 44% said to work hard.

4. 33% said to challenge yourself.

5. 30% said to become an expert.

6. 26% said to align with your passion.

7. 21% said to be in right space (heart of the action).

8. 16% said to be humble.

9. 9% gave other reasons.

It would be easy to take the top three to say that these are the commonalities, and two of which are pillars, but the one thing that everyone had most in common was that their answers are more or less unique to them.

When you think about it, it's not surprising. The answer given nearly always relates to what made that person successful. After all, it is what they know best.

To take it a step further, are there commonalities in those who become Elite faster than others? Interestingly, yes! The research does appear to support that view.

If you dig further into the data and evaluate the correlation between how long someone has been in full-time work, in sales, whether they have always been in sales, the year they became Elite and whether they graduated from university, it reveals interesting insights.

Table 3: Statistics relating to the 50 research participants' careers:

CHARACTERISTIC	YEARS	CHARACTERISTIC	PERCENTAGE
In full-time work	14.16	Went to university	82%
In sales	12.24	Only worked in sales	64%
In another discipline	1.92		
To become Elite in sales career	5.24		
To become Elite in career	7.16		

For me, I became Elite in the sixth year in my career. As happy as I am to be above average, I'm only just about average in the Elite. If I could give the younger me this book, perhaps the result might have been different!

From the primary group it was possible to identify three more groups:

1. Those who became Elite in their sales career after six years.

2. Those who became Elite in their sales career in five years or fewer.

3. Those who became Elite in their sales career in three years or fewer.

In which case, why the third group? The average of the second group was three years, so it made sense to dig a little deeper and Table 4 shows why that was important.

Table 4: The statistics compared

	ALL	UNDER 3	UNDER 5	OVER 6
Full-time work (years)	14.16	12.9	12.0	17.1
In sales (years)	12.24	9.6	9.9	15.5
Not in sales (years)	1.92	3.3	2.1	1.6
Elite in sales (years)	5.24	2.4	3.2	8.1
Elite in career (years)	7.16	5.7	5.3	9.7
University (percentage)	82%	100%	93%	66%
Only sales (percentage)	64%	41%	62%	66%

KEY TRENDS:

- People who spent more of their career not in sales, became Elite in their sales career faster.

- People who became Elite in their career faster were more likely to have graduated from university.

- The time to become Elite in a sales career has sped up.

When you then explore the answers the Elite salespeople gave on their advice to aspirational salespeople, Table 5 shows some insightful takeaways.

Table 5: Elite salespeople's key advice for success

	ALL	UNDER 3	UNDER 5	OVER 6
Learning	65%	53%	60%	72%
Mentors	49%	47%	44%	56%
Hard work	44%	33%	44%	44%
Challenge	33%	33%	32%	33%
Expert	30%	47%	36%	22%
Passion	26%	20%	20%	33%
Right space	21%	40%	32%	6%
Be humble	16%	13%	24%	6%
Other	9%	0%	0%	22%

KEY TRENDS:

- Those who become Elite faster place a greater emphasis on being an expert.

- Those who become Elite faster place a greater emphasis on being in the right space.

- Those who become Elite faster place less emphasis on learning.

Amongst the other statistics, there are some interesting insights to pull out, although no true trends. For example, those who became Elite in their sales career in three years or fewer are the only group that places less emphasis on hard work. Perhaps they knew something the others did not!

To explore this point further, those who become Elite faster believe that being in the right space (a pillar) and being an expert in what you do (a pillar) are key things aspirational salespeople should focus on. People in this group also spent the longest time outside of sales compared with the other groups. Often, they started their career in relatable roles such as consultancy or project management.

So, not only in the research project were the pillars validated, but it also identified the fastest way to become Elite in a sales career.

Which is to:

- graduate from university;

- become a specialist in a field in the heart of the action that you are passionate about;

- after 3.3 years join a tech company that sells a high-value solution to enterprises in this space;

- align yourself with the right mentors; and

- learn how to sell.

In 2.4 years, you will have a very good chance of being an Elite salesperson.

Wouldn't it have been fantastic to receive that advice early in life? Or, if you are at the start of your career, re-read that paragraph until it's imprinted on your mind!

However, try to tell the young Justin Golding, Ben Tunstall, Brendan McLaughlin or even me that we had to go to university for fast success in sales. Individually we would have all laughed at you and made it our mission to prove you wrong! The first thing we all wanted to do was to sell; we love it and we've excelled because of that passion.

Equally, for Jefferson Mangus, university meant that he got to spend a year abroad in Copenhagen, Denmark, where he met his wife and had his first stab at entrepreneurship.

For Madeline Storr, it meant she got to work in Berlin and Paris for a year and gain her first true exposure to corporate sales, which she loved. Admittedly, she didn't enjoy the study aspect of university, but admits that the overall experience set her up for life afterwards.

If Philip Nyborg had not attended university, he might not have developed his passion for technology and gone on to build a solid network at IBM, which immeasurably set him up for success.

These people would have gone to university regardless; the pillars wouldn't have mattered to them as they had their own reasons for going. More to the point, they had no idea they would become a salesperson on completing their studies.

In life we all take our own journeys for reasons personal to us and, at times, for reasons out of our control. We develop differently, which opens unique opportunities in life as we step forward.

The establishment of the pillars in our careers is no different.

Marcus almost took a different career path after he graduated, but when he walked through the doors at Finsda and met his future mentors, it connected with him. He believed his ambition to become highly successful could happen there. To start with, he knew very little and found himself in tough environments. The first thing that helped him progress was having mentors. They saw him as their prodigy and supported his development. As his confidence grew, he stepped outside of his comfort zone, studied the financial markets, sales skills, and constantly refined his work. In his organisation he identified a path to progress his career, set his goals, then delivered and excelled. Step by step, he established himself as an expert and built his skills; his success followed and the momentum carried him. Marcus became Elite in less than three years.

Mandy Smithson has always been the type of person who is energised from talking with others. She loved university. At the start of her career she knew that she wanted to be in a profession where she could get out of the office and meet people. That first job was print ad sales for a national Dutch newspaper. Shortly after starting this job, the industry went through enormous digital disruption. Demand shifted from traditional ads in media such as print, radio and television, to digital ads. Mandy carefully plotted her path to benefit from this disruption. Rather than remaining focussed on print ads, she moved her focus to digital, then programmatic ad campaigns, and finally to the technology that powers the industry.

She became entrenched in her industry and her expertise continued to develop, both of which she loved just as much as talking with people. When she joined major tech companies such as Oracle and Salesforce, she gained new mentors which helped her to rapidly develop her sales skills. Mandy became Elite in fewer than five years, but more than three.

The key takeaway from this is to find what works for you. We are all born individuals and as we grow in life, we establish ourselves. This is what it means to be authentic in sales. This is what happens when you simultaneously build the pillars in your career. Which is why the answers Elite salespeople give to aspirational salespeople are individual to them.

Now let's take this focus back to you. You've read the stories of 17 different Elite salespeople, who started at the bottom and made it to the top of their game. You've read what the pillars are and how Elite salespeople developed these within their own career; this knowledge is only valuable if you implement it in your own career.

Let us first recap on the pillars.

1. Be in the heart of the action.

Where there is considerable disruption and innovation, there is money to invest. The bigger the disruption, the bigger the opportunity, and therefore, the bigger the budgets.

As a salesperson this is where you want to be, but it's not only about the market; placing yourself in the right company that will come out on top is a key to success. Don't be on the losing team.

These waves of innovation and disruption often last for many years, so it doesn't matter if you are not there at the start. In fact, if you are there too early it isn't necessarily a smart move. The market needs to be ready. As salespeople we need velocity in our market; high demand means big sales pipelines and big sales pipelines, if managed well, lead to big sales performances, thus big commissions.

2. Be an expert

Being in the heart of the action isn't enough.

To build trust in your prospects and also your own organisation, you need to be an expert in your given space, be that product, industry, vertical—or all three.

When you sell to organisations, buyers look for people who can expertly advise them, so when you meet these expectations it builds trust and that trust will help you to secure business.

Your expert status will also have an impact internally; if you know what you're talking about, your colleagues will turn to you for advice and your leaders will trust you to deliver. When you seek new roles, this credibility will set you apart.

3. Be a student of sales

Even though it is important to be an expert, and that will set you apart from other salespeople, you are still a salesperson. It is your responsibility to bring in business. Just like being successful as a lawyer, doctor, accountant, a tradesperson or any other profession, if you want to be successful in sales, you must develop your skills.

Sales is a profession, and to be successful as a salesperson there is a wide range of skills you must learn and that is exactly the point. Commit yourself to being a student of sales.

As you progress through your career and move on to more complex sales with larger average order values, there is always more to learn. Another thing to be aware of is that buyer mentalities change. As a seller, we must keep up, we must keep developing.

Take sales methodologies seriously, read sales books, listen to podcasts, take company training, attend workshops and so on. Doing so will lead to a greater level of success.

4. Be the master of your own destiny

Ambition to be successful and owning your career are two separate things. Any successful person in any field takes ownership of their path and plots their way to success. This might be a formal career plan, with clear goals that lead them to their big goals. Or it could be an awareness of the opportunities around them and making their move to capitalise on them before others. Or, the very best approach is to do both.

In sales, as an individual contributor, there is a natural career path, even though not every company offers this. It is ingrained in the industry. The career path starts where the sales process does, with pipeline generation; the top end is closing business. As your skillset develops you work bigger deals and sell to bigger businesses.

The above paragraph pretty much sums it up. Within it, the following roles apply:

- Business/Sales Development Representative (BDR/SDR)—SME, mid-market or enterprise.

- Account/Sales executive—SME, mid-market or enterprise.

- Strategic/Global account manager (GAM)/Major account executive—these exist at the very largest global companies.

Companies' definitions of the boundaries vary, but those are the foundations of an individual contributor's sales career.

Elite salespeople operate at the higher end of this spectrum. To become Elite, you must plot your path; it is your responsibility alone. Sometimes you can achieve it within one organisation, sometimes you must work for several. The important point is that you make it to the top.

5. Mentorship

The fastest and most effective way to learn anything is through the experience of others. Mentorship is the last pillar because it applies to all the other pillars.

A key thing to remember is that when you receive advice from someone who has achieved the thing you have set out to accomplish, big or small, it is mentorship. They will shape the guidance they give you based on their own experiences. Advice received from several people gives you a broader view and helps you to develop faster.

As we move through life, the mentors we have change and it's important that they do; it's a marker you've reached the next level in your personal development. Some people get formal mentors; most ask for ad hoc advice. Formal mentors are more effective, but harder to find. To find them, aim high and go for it. Fear of rejection holds most people back, even the Elite.

6.The underlying principle, authenticity

When you establish the pillars, you will naturally form an authentic brand that sets you apart from the rest. This is not a pillar, but what results from establishing the pillars.

THEORY INTO PRACTICE

Throughout the book, at the end of each chapter, advice is provided on how you can establish and grow that pillar in your career. The establishment of the pillars is not like erecting a tower. Once a tower is built, it is a tower, it's a structure, it will remain that way unless otherwise altered.

Establishing the pillars is like growing a forest: when the seeds of nature settle, over the seasons and years they turn into saplings, then into small trees, and one day trees that touch the sky. If trees are left untouched, they continue to grow.

Perhaps throughout this book you paused at the end of each chapter and thought long and hard about how you could grow that given pillar in your career, or perhaps you plan to read the book to the end and then decide. Whichever way you approach this, the decision is yours, the knowledge and lessons are within. This is your path and however you establish the pillars in your career will shape the person you become. Which, when you think about it, is exciting, right?

Time to put theory into practice. Don't build a tower—grow a forest.

CHAPTER 9

BE THE CORPORATE ATHLETE

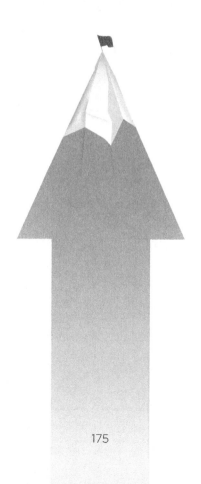

06:00

10:30

18:30

We salespeople get a huge buzz when we secure a deal. It's what keeps us on our toes, but if that deal also propels us to the top of the leaderboard or delivers our yearly target, it magnifies the buzz!

The wildest times to be on a sales floor are in the days running up to the end of the financial year. You'll see people elevated to new heights almost crying tears of happiness, or on the flip side you'll see people crushed as they fail to secure the sales required to deliver their yearly target. It's quite something!

On a more extreme spectrum, imagine a striker in a football (soccer) team in the World Cup. Picture every stride they take, each touch of the ball, their country behind them, cheering them on to bring home the trophy. As they line up the shot with precise intentions of hitting the back of the net, the fans freeze in anticipation.

A goal?

It's a goal! The fans scream in applause and their opponent crumbles in despair!

A save or miss? The attacking team's fans fall to their knees in despair whilst the defending team rises in triumph.

If this is the final or at the end of the game, the buzz is magnified. Athletes and salespeople alike share a love of the buzz of success.

In fact, it's not uncommon to find athletes in the sales profession. Ryan Chapman had an opportunity to play Rugby for New Zealand before he pursued a career in sales. Brendan McLaughlin was a talented football player, but decided it wasn't the career for him. And Mandy Smithson is a regular marathon runner.

Both professions have leagues. In the championship leagues of sport you will find the athletes we all know and love (or sometimes hate!). In sales, the top championship leagues are where you'll find Elite salespeople. Before athletes of either profession reach the championship leagues, they start at the bottom, in the amateur leagues. Determination and raw talent are probably all they have at this stage. After early signs of success, they'll probably be noticed and offered an opportunity to progress in their paths to the top. To continue this pace, they must develop their skills and become the best amongst their peers. Endless hours, days, weeks and years of training is what it takes. But even when you've developed your skills to the highest level, success is not guaranteed. This isn't just the act of doing, it is a mindset. Too often we witness the remarkable achievements of others, but do we know and truly appreciate what happens behind the scenes?

MUHAMMAD ALI

Muhammad Ali is renowned as one of the greatest boxing legends. Achievements such as winning the World Heavyweight title three times and being the first person in history to do so, earnt him his spot. He had 61 fights in his professional career, with a record of 56 wins, 37 knockouts and 5 losses. But Ali's life was far from easy.

He was born in Louisville, Kentucky in 1942 with the birth name Cassius Clay, when segregation and racism were a major part of day-to-day life.[1] Young Cassius felt the pain first-hand, even being denied food at grocery stores because of his skin colour as a black male.

At age twelve, someone stole his beloved bike. He reported it to his local police officer, Joe Martin, and declared he would beat the person who did this. Joe Martin looked at the young, very wired Cassius Clay, ready to explode, and responded that he'd need to learn how to fight first, which came as a surprise for Clay, I am sure. Outside of his police duties, Joe Martin was a boxing coach and took the young boy under his wing.[2]

Cassius Clay became completely committed to training hard, day and night. He hated every minute of it, but said to himself:

'Don't quit. Suffer now and live the rest of your life as a champion'.

By the age of 18, Clay had won two national Golden Gloves titles, two Amateur Athletic Union national titles and had achieved 100 wins versus 8 losses.

His achievements and commitment to the sport did not go unnoticed, and after graduating from high school, he travelled to Rome in Italy and represented the U.S. in light heavyweight boxing for the 1960 Summer Olympics. He returned with the gold medal and as a national hero. His fast footwork and powerful jab had been too much for his opponents.

I'm not sure if he ever found the person who stole his bike, but if he did, I'm sure you could have added that as a win to his record!

Shortly after the Olympics, Clay debuted as a professional, winning his first fight by way of decision followed by 19 further wins, which included 15 knock-outs. This gave him the opportunity for his first title shot on February 25th, 1964, against reigning British heavyweight champion, Sonny Liston. Clay relentlessly taunted Liston before the fight, famously promising to *'float like a butterfly, sting like a bee'* and predicting a knockout. After a relentless battle, Liston could not start the seventh round and Clay was crowned Heavyweight Champion of the World. He roared, *'I am the greatest!'*[3]

In March of 1964, Clay converted to Islam and was renamed Muhammad Ali. The Vietnam War was raging and the U.S. government enlisted many fit men to pick up arms. They enlisted Muhammad Ali in 1967, but he refused. This was against his religious beliefs and he would not fight. They stripped Ali of his boxing licence and belts, ordering him to pay a $10,000 fine and sentenced him to five years in prison. Many fans deserted him. Yet he could fortunately live as a free man whilst he appealed the conviction. This happened at the height of his career, when he should have been showing that he was indeed the great-est. His new fight was to quash the conviction. Three years later, the public was behind him and by 1970 he could reclaim his boxing licence. Only one thing was on his mind: get back in the ring and reclaim his titles.

In October 1971 during Ali's first fight back he dealt a devastating knock-out to Jerry Quay in round three, which secured him a fight to reclaim his belts against the feared reigning champion Joe Frazier, who had been in the ascen-dant whilst Ali had been out of the ring. On 8th March 1971 the titans clashed. Ali was floored with a left hook by Frazier in the last round, stumbled back to his feet, only to lose the fight by a unanimous decision. Frazier remained cham-pion! The fight earned the title 'Fight of the Century'.[4]

Failure in a comeback for many boxers can lead to a decline in their career, yet Ali rose to the challenge and won his next ten fights to rebuild his unstop-pable reputation. Ken Norton put a stop to that when he stunned spectators and defeated Ali. Unsurprisingly, Ali refused to give up and secured a rematch. He defeated Norton six months later, adding momentum towards reclaiming his belts. If he were to win his next fight, he would be the mandatory challenger to reclaim the belts. By now, the world champion was George Foreman, who had defeated Joe Frazier. Ali's next fight would be with a familiar opponent, a rematch with the feared Joe Frazier.

Such a rematch deserved a grand title, the 'Thrilla in Manila', and it almost went the distance. Both men took serious punishment! Frazier was worse, which led his trainer to throw in the towel at round 14. Ali had not only secured his title shot but had his revenge against Frazier.[5]

The 'Rumble in the Jungle', a fight held in Kinshasa, Zaire, would go down in the history books. Ali was considered the underdog against the formidable and undefeated George Foreman, who was a massive, powerful boxer. The performance by Ali was like none the world had seen. Ali taunted Foreman into throwing wild punches while he ducked and bounced off the ropes to avoid their impact. This became known as the 'rope-a-dope' technique, which tired the mighty Foreman. As the fight dragged on, Ali dealt a shocking knockout in the eighth round, leading Harry Carpenter to exclaim: *'Oh my God, he's won the title back at 32!'*[6]

During the years that followed, the trio battled it out and some upcoming legendary boxers entered the ring. Most notable was Leon Spinks, who defeated Ali in 1978 after a 15-round split decision, which to nobody's surprise, Ali avenged and reclaimed the belts in a rematch seven months later. Fans of the sport refer to this period as the 'Golden age of heavyweight boxing'.

There are few stories out there with so many highs and lows. No matter the cards that were dealt, Muhammad Ali got back up, dusted himself off and fought for his dream to be the greatest of all time. However, the fight wasn't just in the ring. He had to deal with racism, political struggles, intense training regimes and short recovery periods between his brutal battles with some of the greatest heavyweight boxers the world has ever seen. This is more than doing: this is believing, this is the mindset of a champion—the greatest of all time.

ROGER BANNISTER

Roger Bannister, a man who defied belief to the contrary, did what many considered impossible. On the evening of 6th May 1954 at Oxford Iffley Road track, England, he was the first man in recorded history to run a mile in under 4 minutes when he achieved a time of 3 minutes 59.4 seconds.[7] This is a moment in sports history that will never be forgotten and which continues to inspire many athletes to this day.

Other than the thrill, there were a couple of motivators that led young Bannister to take up running. First, he wanted to avoid the local bullies and second, to avoid the rain of Nazi bombs and machine guns during World War II. He was a young boy during the Battle of Britain. The eerie sound of sirens is something he'd never forget. Perhaps this fear gave him strength in his races.[8]

He grew up in Harrow, London. Fortunately for Bannister, he and his family fled to Bath during the worst of the Blitz. Upon their return, he started school and it disappointed him to learn that they did not consider running a competitive sport. The focus was on rowing and rugby.

Throughout school Bannister dreamt of going into medicine. He graduated with good grades to earn his place at Oxford University and to his delight they valued running. It was here that he picked up a pair of spikes, which changed his life. 4:53, a respectable time, was his first recorded mile at 17, which earnt him a place on the team.

In 1951 Bannister had become a British champion in the mile run and earned his place at the 1952 Helsinki Olympics. He was one of Britain's only hopes to bring home a gold. With a strong start and looking to go to the finals, at the last minute the officials added a semifinal because of the large number of entrants. This disrupted Bannister's planned recovery time, and, depleted, he finished the semifinals in fourth position, eliminating him from the contest. He returned to England shamed and empty-handed. He felt utterly disappointed as he thought he had let his country down.

Yet this defeat would not stop him in his tracks. The following year, in 1953, he once again won the British Championship and set his sights on a greater achievement in 1954's running season. Bannister became determined to beat the four-minute mile. It was now or never. He put his studies to use and became obsessed with the mechanics of running. This knowledge shaped his relentless training scheme that used new scientific methods.

Never being more prepared for anything in his life, on 6th May 1954 at 6pm, he lined up to start the annual Amateur Athletic Association race held at Oxford's Iffley Road track. Bannister held mid-pack throughout the race. With 350 yards left to go, he released his reserves to gain the lead position and secured a time of 3 minutes and 59.4 seconds. The crowd roared in celebration. On that racetrack, he became a national hero.[9]

However, his record was bested only a matter of weeks later. On 21st June 1954, a young Australian man by the name of John Landy lowered the world record to 3 minutes 58 seconds, 1.4 milliseconds faster.[10] There was only one way to settle this, and the two men had to face each other in the next competitive race. It took place at the British Empire and Commonwealth games in Vancouver, British Columbia, on 7th August 1954.[11]

35,000 spectators witnessed the champions compete for glory. Landy led the race with Bannister closely behind and, on the last lap, Bannister chased Landy down to ever so slightly take the lead and win. Both athletes ran the mile in under 3 minutes, Bannister securing his personal best of 3 minutes 58.8 seconds, which was a much more gratifying win as he was up against the most elite opponent in the world. The race became known as the 'Miracle Mile'. Later that year, Bannister retired from competitive running to focus on his studies and medical career, although his love for running never waned.

In later life he continued to achieve a great deal, becoming a Director at the National Hospital for Nervous Diseases in London, serving as the Chairman of the British Sports Council, and, perhaps most notable of all, achieving one of the greatest British honours of all when he was knighted by Queen Elizabeth II to become Sir Roger Gilbert Bannister.

Ali and Bannister are two very different athletes. Yet both shared their fair share of hardships *en route* to achieving their greatest desire of becoming the best in their sport and making their mark in the history books. A clear focus and passion played a major part in their success, but their underlying hard work and grit kept them on track no matter what the world threw at them. We see this mindset in the athletes who inspire the world, as well as in the entrepreneurs and innovators who shape the world.

CORPORATE ATHLETES

The story of the rise of tech shared in Chapter 3 includes many solid examples. Herman Hollerith, an American inventor, developed a machine to calculate and record the data collected in the U.S. census, where the country had experienced a boom in population. It took him ten years to achieve this! Before this, he had secured several smaller projects in the U.S. that proved his machines could dramatically speed up processes, increase accuracy and reduce costs.

Hollerith's success in the U.S. led to machines being installed in Europe and Russia. Later, his company, Tabulating Machine Company, merged with five others to form the Computing Tabulating Recording Company, which later rebranded to IBM. He was one of the true pioneers of the digital computing age. Had Herman Hollerith given up during those ten gruelling years, the world might be very different. Yet something kept him going. Maybe his vision was the computing age? Or perhaps something else. Whatever it was, he was a corporate athlete, no doubt.

The dawn of the digital computing age, largely led by IBM, led to the emergence and dominance of software. A notable antecedent of the mass adoption of this industry was Microsoft, co-founded by Bill Gates and Paul Allen.

Before even founding Microsoft, the two became friends at Lakeside School, Seattle, in the late 1960s, when Gates was in eighth grade and Allen in the tenth. The school had funded a computer terminal, which the young men had become obsessed with. It was expensive at $40 an hour, but they found a bug that allowed them to use it for free. A lot of kids would sneak out at night to go to parties, but Gates and Allen would sneak out to break into the school and use the computer terminal.[12]

This is when they founded their first venture together, Traf-O-Data, which helped their local council to develop a more efficient system to count the number of cars that passed on a road. The pair made a modest income from the project, with Gates only 17 years old and Allen 19. But it wasn't long until the school figured out what they were up to and threatened to close them down! Agreeing a deal with the school, they continued their use of the computer and Traf-O-Data endured for many more years. Eventually, unfortunately, it flopped. They had failed to consider that councils around the country were not comfortable buying a technology system from a bunch of students.[13]

The pair moved on, Allen becoming a software engineer at Honeywell and Gates going on to study at Harvard University. Until one day, Allen urgently rushed Gates to a newspaper stand and showed him the latest news about the Altair Air 8800. He famously said, '*Look, it's happening without us!*'[14]

As much as computers had moved forward, software was still far behind. The men devised an operating system under the name 'Micro-soft'. Rather than building their own computer, they decided a more effective route to market was to partner with the likes of Altair. To their delight, Altair accepted their proposal. The Micro-soft team worked endless nights to ensure they had bug-free software to ship to Altair, which they duly delivered. Altair achieved remarkable success from the collaboration. The company was rebranded Microsoft, which became the operating system for Apple and IBM.

None of this would have happened without the endless nights of hard work, risk-taking and continuous education. With these attributes, the pair are blinding examples of corporate athletes, although I'm sure they would have given themselves the label of 'corporate professionals'. Nonetheless, the traits and behaviours they displayed perfectly matched those displayed by their athlete counterparts.

Let's bring that back to Elite salespeople. All have countless stories to share of the hard graft they had to put in to achieve success.

You may remember Phil Nyborg, the Dane who knew that he wanted to get into IT from a young age and quickly achieved success in his sales career. Note that Phil had his own challenges!

In Scandinavian countries, because of the long winters with little sunlight, it's universally accepted to take July as a holiday. One summer Phil was responsible for a highly competitive RFP for a strategic deal while working at IBM. July struck and his friends, family and colleagues disappeared for the summer. Phil did not. He continued to graft, determined to win the deal. If he did, it would make him the top salesperson for the year.

Six months into the sales cycle, Phil had IBM shortlisted as one of two vendors. He was sure that he would win. Shortly after, he received news that struck him to the core. Despite the value add of IBM, the prospect couldn't justify the 23% price premium and selected the other vendor. This stopped him in his tracks. For the first time in Phil's career, he missed his sales target. Devastated, and struggling to accept what happened, Phil considered leaving the sales profession.

He took some time to reflect, dusted himself off and realised where he went wrong. He got carried away; he got overly excited at the size of the deal and hadn't properly qualified the opportunity; he shouldn't have pursued it the way that he did. This lesson Phil never forgot, and he was soon back on the high-performance track.

The following year he had one of his best sales performances and his success increased year on year. Hard work, graft and dedication are the keys to his success.

Haig Hanessian, from a young age, was determined to become a successful salesperson. His grandfather had inspired him as a boy, when he showed Haig around his factories outside of Mexico City. The words he never forgot were, *'None of this starts without sales.'*

He started his sales career selling building materials and later moved to insurance sales. The first year in which Haig finally became Elite, he earnt $145,000, had three jobs and worked all hours of the clock. With a pregnant wife, he could just about maintain the pace.

This was unsustainable, which led him to transition to a U.S. SaaS company called Open Table that had expanded into Mexico. He learnt that he could make similar money, but work fewer hours. Although the Mexican market was behind the U.S. and despite building some momentum, it wasn't at the same level of success he'd previously achieved. He left Open Table, with only minimal sales success.

Insurance sales called him back to lead a team. Haig soon got himself back on track. He thought this was it. This is where his career would be. Some time later he caught up with a successful friend who worked for SAP in Enterprise tech sales. This friend earned more money than anyone else he knew! Intrigued, Haig showed interest in joining SAP, but his friend told him it was too late in his career to make that transition. Rather than knocking him back, it motivated Haig; he accepted the challenge, got a position at SAP, grafted to become an expert and rose to the top of the sales board.

His journey taught him all that he needed to become Elite, and from the very start his mindset was that of a corporate athlete and still is to this day.

On the surface, often we just see the successes of others and do not always truly appreciate the graft they put in, to be where they are. Yet when you examine the story of success, hard work is always present; it is the glue of success. To be elite in anything is more than just skill, it is more than being in the right place at the right time (although that's important), it is more than having someone to guide you. Being elite is about your mindset.

Sales is not a nine-to-five job, it is rather the type of job where you'll do whatever it takes to overachieve your number and use your momentum to get promoted to sell higher-value products to earn bigger commissions. To move to better, faster-growing companies with more opportunities. To secure more senior titles and every step along the way, year by year, increase your take-home. Or one day even start your own business.

Elite salespeople have the mindsets of champions, to rise to the very top in what it is they do and not to stop when they get there. There is no glass ceiling; they smash through ceilings. If it won't smash, they find another way around.

Do you have the mindset to be Elite?

Do you have the mindset to be a corporate athlete?

By now, if reading this book has helped you to learn the pillars of an Elite sales career and you've used that knowledge to build your own individual career plan, you should have designed a path to become an Elite salesperson.

To now establish the pillars in your career, it requires you to be a corporate athlete. This is not another pillar; it is a necessary behaviour and mindset.

Do not give up when the going gets tough. Do not let that key deal you lost stop you in your tracks. Do not let that month, quarter or year when you did not hit target deter you from the profession. Take every failure as a lesson, pick yourself up, refocus and hit it harder until you overcome this obstacle in front of you. When you do, you'll know what it feels like to be a corporate athlete.

Madeline Storr treats every loss as an opportunity and she has had her fair share. She conducts a post-mortem every time she loses a deal to identify how she can succeed next time. That continuous focus allowed her to become a global top salesperson at Salesforce.

Success will not come easy, but when it does, it will come fast. If you stay on track, your success will compound, and as it compounds, it will take you to your destination. The only person stopping you is you!

The only way to establish the pillars in your career, with a sound plan in place and to achieve the ambitious goals you set yourself, is to be a corporate athlete. It means everything!

Develop this mindset and don't stop until you've achieved what you set out to do.

CHAPTER 10

THE JOURNEY
IS THE REWARD

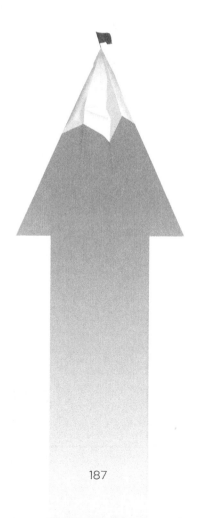

On planet Earth, there are few things that unite all humans. One is that we have a limited amount of time to breathe the air, soak up the sun, spend time with our loved ones and enjoy every moment that we can. The reason for our existence has been a debate across the ages, but what has remained clear is that our time is limited. It's commonly known that when a person is approaching the end of their life, it is rare for them to say, '*I wish I had made more money*', or '*I wish I had indulged more in luxury items*', or '*I wish I had got that last promotion at work*'.

People will more likely say, '*I wish I had shown my love to my partner and cherished my time with them*', or '*I wish I had spent more time with my children as they grew up and was a better parent*', or, '*I wish I had travelled the world*', or, '*I wish I had spent more time with my friends and built long-lasting relationships.*'

People cherish memories and experiences above all. Our work and money does not care for us the way our loved ones do. It's important we use our time wisely.

This book is for those who desire to build an Elite sales career, perform at the highest level and achieve remarkable success. This book is for the corporate athlete. High-performing people are prepared to do whatever it takes to succeed. We are prepared to work ourselves into the ground; when we drop we get back up and when we tire we keep pushing. We do not stop until we have succeeded.

Success could be to provide for your family. To some that might mean a lifestyle of dreams, a big house with a large garden on a sought-after road, several breath-taking holidays a year, private education for your children and luxury cars that roar as you turn the ignition. A lifestyle without financial constraints.

Success could be to provide for yourself. Financial success affords us the luxury to do as we wish on many fronts. Regular long weekends to any destination that takes our desire, annual beach and ski holidays, designer goods, or drinking and dining at the most sought-after establishments.

Some people are more interested in how they invest their money. Property, stocks, angel investments, or others could be their goals. Wealth gives us the foundation to guarantee our security in life as we go forward and prepare for many eventualities.

Our success could be furthering charitable causes. Whether that is by donations of money or of your time to causes close to your heart.

Most likely your goals are a combination of those mentioned and more. Whatever it is, it doesn't matter; what matters is that it is important to you. Individually, we will do what it takes to achieve our goals, as this is what drives us. Yet, as admirable as the traits are of a corporate athlete, they can pose a threat to our health.

Perhaps you exercise regularly, eat well and your body shows that you are a healthy person. The threat I refer to is not physical health, it is mental. The core function that keeps our brain in a positive place that allows us to perform at the level required of us.

When we continually push ourselves, and focus all our energies on being successful, there is less time to do the things that make us happy, and over time (if we believe it or not) this wears us down. As life throws the challenges it does at us, we become weaker and weaker, less capable of handling it in a way we might have otherwise. All because we didn't focus on what truly makes us happy. Above all, we cannot get back the time we lost.

As the classic saying goes, *'All work and no play makes Jack a dull boy'*.

At the extreme end of this spectrum, I am referring to burnout. This is when we, and our environments, push ourselves so hard that, rather than motivating us to achieve more, it has a negative effect on our performance. We become depleted, unable to focus, overwhelmed and in more severe cases, depressed. It is the occupational risk high-performance people must face.

For a very long time people believed burnout to be only a buzzword, coined in 1974 by Herbert Freudenberger, a German-born American psychologist. It wasn't until May 2019 the World Health Organization and the International

Classification of Diseases (ICD-11) had officially recognised burnout as an 'occupational phenomenon'. They describe burnout as '*a syndrome conceptualized as resulting from chronic workplace stress that has not been successfully managed.*'[1]

Three symptoms can help you recognise it:

- A depletion of energy and exhaustion.

- An increase in mental distance from the job and negative sentiment about one's job.

- Poorer performance at work.

Burnout refers specifically to phenomena in the occupational context and does not apply to other experiences in life.

As a salesperson you will have targets to achieve and, as you progress in your career, those targets typically get bigger. Failure to perform leads to the slippery slope and failing to reach your own goals, which hurts more. This pressure is always there.

To be successful, we must work harder than everyone else and are expected to perform. This over time can lead to chronic workplace stress. How we manage that is up to us and managing it well is important in order not to lead to a decline in our mental wellbeing.

HOW BIG A PROBLEM IS THIS?

In 2018, Gallup released a study they had completed on nearly 7,500 full-time employees and found that 23% of employees reportedly burned out at work often or always. An additional 44% reported burnout sometimes.[2]

That means about two-thirds of full-time workers experience burnout on the job.

There are no details on the breakdown of job roles and industries. Many consider sales as one of the most stressful positions within an organisation. If two-thirds of employees overall experience burnout on the job, you can imagine it will be just as high if not higher for salespeople. Most consider salespeople to be strong-minded. We are on the front line every day and have thick skin from handling constant rejection, which is largely true. But we as salespeople are still human, there is no escaping that, as much we sometimes try. Burnout is to be taken seriously.

My belief is that the most effective way to avoid burnout is to focus on our happiness, the present, the moment and what deeply satisfies us.

Throughout learning the pillars you may have noticed a key theme is to focus on what matters to you. Whether that be industry, technology or goals. There is a simple reason behind this; it's all related to your happiness.

Gallup discovered that when people are inspired, motivated and supported in their work, they do more work, and that work is significantly less stressful on their overall health and wellbeing.[3] Even when you find your sweet spot, if you work all the hours of the day, it will wear you down. Life is more than chasing success; we must prioritise happiness. Yet it can be complex. Happiness is when we feel fantastic about life and cannot help but smile, and this energy enables us to perform at our absolute best.

By nature our wants and desires are similar, as are the things that make us happy. We can divide the components of happiness into several areas of life:

Love—family, friends, partners

Career—success, progression, feeling of doing something meaningful

Financial—basic needs, lifestyle, investments, financial security

Adventure—travel, outdoors, new experiences

Health—fitness, healthy eating, mental wellbeing

This is by no means a complete list, but it gives us a framework. A complete list would take an enormous study to understand all the different variables for different individuals. A study for another day!

When you consider the different components of happiness in our own individual lives, we can look it at as an equation. With the provided example, let's give each a score of 1–10, 10 being 'couldn't be happier' and 1 being 'couldn't be unhappier'. The equation for happiness is:

When $(L + C + F + A + H) / 5$ is equal or greater to X, you are happy; when it is below X, you are unhappy.

X is X because for you 7 might be happiness, for me that might be 8. I'm sure if we looked at this with a statistically significant sample, we could find some averages. If, for whatever reason, your score is negative for happiness, this can have a direct impact on other areas of life. As an example, let's say your X is 7 and at the current time your happiness score is 7. Imagine that, overnight, a company in which you held 40% of your wealth as stock suffers a decline in stock price of 90% with no sign of recovery. Add to that you were also overweight, not having exercised properly nor eaten well in the past six months. The combined effect of these negative events reduces your happiness score from 7 to 6.4.

Two weeks later you lose a deal at work, which in most scenarios you'd accept, learn from and move on. But because you are already in a negative place, which might have influenced why you lost the deal, the news of this loss hits you hard and you struggle to accept the news. A negative decline ensues on your Financial and Career scores. The low 6.4 happiness score slides down to 5.9.

The pressure on you at work increases and you work even harder. You miss several social events and upset a friend. Workplace stress further increases. This is the path to burnout.

Burnout is specifically related to chronic workplace stress, however the causes and preventions of stress in the workplace exist in all areas of life. It is your responsibility to do your very best to be aware of this and manage it, before it gets the better of you.

Take a moment.

What's important for you in life? What makes you happy? What is your equation for happiness?

Maybe a key thing for you is your health. There might be a certain sport you love to do or, perhaps staying fit and healthy is what matters to you. How does it make you feel if you are succeeding or failing in this area of life?

Perhaps you are a social person: you love to spend time with friends and family, share memories, being there to support people, taking part in social events and more. How does it make you feel when your life is full of social experiences, or lacking them?

The world is an enormous place and year by year it becomes better connected. Seeing the world and understanding different cultures has become increasingly important for people. From the tropical forests of Latin America, the plains of Africa or the exotic marine life found in the impressive reefs of Asia, the world is full of wonders. How does it make you feel when you spread your wings or stay confined to your local area?

Whatever it is, how complex or simple, be sure of it.

When you embrace life in all the areas that matter to you, it keeps your happiness score equal to or greater than your X, which results in keeping a smile on your face. The energy that powers that smile is what will keep you in a positive mindset, which enables you to perform at the highest level in all areas of life. Elite salespeople are very aware of this.

Justin Golding from a young age placed his career above all else. This focus propelled his career and financial status to an impressive place. As he approached his late twenties, he met the lady he wanted to marry and build a family with, which increasingly became more important for him.

These realisations amplified whilst he was a VP of Sales for Lead Forensics, where he directly led a sales team of over 100, including 10 sales managers and 3 senior sales managers. For him to continue this job, he had to sacrifice time in his personal life. It gradually grated on his happiness. Justin dreamed of one day being able to walk his child to school in the morning and of providing a financially stable lifestyle for his family. This desire led Justin to become an enterprise account executive rather than a VP of Sales of SMB sales teams. The transition was not smooth, had many bumps in the road, but eventually he got it just right at SalesLoft. Here he performed as one of the top enterprise salespeople globally, which allowed him to build the lifestyle he envisioned. Justin is not just an Elite salesperson, he is someone that focusses on his happiness.

Ryan Chapman from a young age dreamt of nothing more than being a pilot. Throughout his younger years and university he trained to be the best pilot he could be, focussing on aerobatics in particular.

In the years of his education and those that followed post-graduation, Ryan met many pilots and gained a glimpse into what this lifestyle means. They spend most of their working life in the cockpit, live hotel to hotel and leave little time for family and friends. This wasn't the life he wanted. Though Ryan dreamt of being a pilot, he also wanted to have a family and a buzzing social life, something that he always held dear when growing up. This realisation and his experiences in his first sales job led him to change the course of his career and become a salesperson rather than a pilot. His happiness made him change his mind. Fortunately, the career path he chose pays very well, particularly as Ryan has achieved a lot of success. He continues to fly planes, but as a hobby. Rather than his passion being his career, his passion remains a hobby.

Fast forward ten years from that decision, and Ryan has a loving wife, a young son of whom he couldn't be prouder, is a fantastic aerobatics pilot in his spare time, and a highly successful enterprise salesperson. The decision he made at a relatively young age—to focus on his happiness—had a profound impact on his life. Something I am sure he thanks his younger self for.

Now to share a final story with you, that to be honest when I started this book, I did not think I would. However, this personal story has an important life lesson.

As shared at the beginning of the book, I first achieved consistent success in my sales career at a B2B web analytics company called Lead Forensics. It was very much a cutthroat sales culture. The Managing Director liked to create scenes of the famous film '*The Wolf of Wall Street*' in the sales office, which to be honest was a lot of fun! At 21, all I wanted was success.

Mentors helped me to realise that sales is a skill you must learn and guided me to sales books, sales training courses, you name it. Every working day from 7.30am to 9am I spent my time studying at my desk in the office.

The amount of effort I put in at work directly translated into sales statistics, such as meetings booked, demos sat, proposals out and deals closed. So I worked 9am to 7pm every day. During business hours I would be on the phone, then after hours I did my admin from the day and prepared for the next.

Fitness was always important to me and at the time I got into a training regime called CrossFit, which is a combination of Olympic weightlifting and HIIT. It's one of the most intense training programmes out there. Training three-to-four times a week, I became addicted. It made me feel fantastic—after the workout, not during, as that was hell. Then, every weekend I partied hard with my friends.

Before all of this I worked normal working hours, went to the gym to lift weights, had fun on the weekends and achieved fairly good results at work.

This transformation of lifestyle was over a few short months; I went from a casual jog to a full-on sprint. It drained me, but I continued to push as there was nothing I wanted more than to be successful.

My sales results showed a sharp increase and I received a lot of praise at work. My physique massively improved, which kept my girlfriend of the time happy and the weekends were a lot of fun. I felt unstoppable.

During a tough day, I arrived at CrossFit to do what they warned was one of the most brutal workouts in recent times. Of my 20 fellow athletes (as we liked to call ourselves) I started slowly, but pushed on and focussed on my own results. Those who used their energy early struggled as the workout continued and my continued pace pushed me past them. I remember a pure tunnel vision in this workout. Only one thing mattered: finishing.

The torture continued and to my amazement, as someone relatively new to the sport, I finished in the top five. I was buzzing at my achievement. But my first focus was to get my breath back, although I couldn't...

A few short moments after the workout, I dropped to my knees and then collapsed. I had a cardiac arrest. My heart stopped beating on the spot. Clinically, I died.

Two of the CrossFit trainers were firemen and knew CPR inside out. There was also a doctor amongst our ranks. The three instantly kicked into action, kept my heart functioning and my blood flowing as the ambulance raced from the UK's No. 1 cardiac hospital, University Hospital, Southampton.

Thirteen minutes later I was resuscitated with a defibrillator by a paramedic, carefully lifted into the back of an ambulance on a stretcher and instantly put into an induced coma. During such traumas the body goes into survival mode and will use all of its energy to remove you from danger. As my brain had been starved of oxygen for 13 minutes, I was at high risk of severe brain damage. The induced coma allows the brain to recover.

After 3 minutes of a cardiac arrest, the chances of someone's survival drops by 50%. As mine lasted 13 minutes, according to the stats I had a 0.2% chance of survival. For whatever reason, my guardian angel looked after me that day.

Two weeks later, after recovering from a five-day coma, loss of memory, complete loss of mental and physical strength, and more examinations than I could possibly tell you, I left the hospital a healthy man. The craziest thing is that I have no underlying heart condition. From what the doctors discovered, my heart is perfectly healthy, without defects. They implanted a small cardiac defibrillator on top of my left pectoral muscle, under the skin. If this ever happens again, the defibrillator will fire and save me.

The clearest memory I have from this period was about day seven, after I had awoken from my coma and my memory returned. For the first couple of days I was a shell of a person, awake for only a few moments every hour.

It was a lovely sunny day, my bed was upright, and I woke to the sun shining on me. On my lap lay a note. As I read the note, written by my Mum, it told the story of what had happened. My memory flooded back and I became emotional. It was like someone had pulled out the rug underneath my feet, with no guarantees of a continued healthy life.

As I calmed, I asked myself, '*Why me?*'

As humans, I think we naturally seek meaning in what has happened to us to make peace in our minds. I continued this train of thought. I believed that I was the type of person trying to make something of myself. Why do I need this lesson? The further I dug, the more the answer became apparent.

Fast forward life on a path of chasing nothing but success. After you achieve the goals in front of you, you do not stop there; you refocus and go on to the next. One day you may achieve outstanding financial and business success, but then what? If you spent your entire life only chasing success, it would lead to emptiness. My lesson from this episode is to no matter what, enjoy the moment, enjoy every second of life, otherwise what is the point?

As an ambitious person, yes, set goals and do whatever it takes to achieve them. But the success part is short-lived and, once achieved, you will pursue another goal. We spend the vast majority of life in the pursuit of things. If you do not find happiness in the pursuit, arguably you throw away an enormous part of your life. After much soul-searching, that is the lesson I took from this and a life lesson I believe all pursuers of success should hold dearly.

Upon full recovery, my ambition remained. My work ethic was still there, although I built myself up slowly, realising you can't go from 5mph to 100mph and continue at that pace for a sustained period.

From that point onward, as much as I focussed on success, I also focussed on enjoying the moment and I was instantly more successful. My sales numbers consistently excelled, my pay increased, I got promoted, my lifestyle was on a different level, I was fit and healthy and enjoyed life at every turn. I focussed on my happiness. Career and success are only one component of that.

What happened to me remains diagnosed as a freak incident. I believe I put too much pressure on myself in all areas of life and my body couldn't handle it as quickly as my mind. This story is on the much more extreme end of burnout and unhappiness, yet the lessons are transferable and clear.

To become an Elite salesperson, the pillars must be built over time. When you take control of establishing the pillars, it accelerates success. Nothing good happens without hard work. On this path, you must be a corporate athlete. However, the hazard of our career path is burnout. It can happen to anyone.

As much as you should focus on your career and do whatever it takes to succeed, you must also focus on what makes you happy so you can operate at your very best and avoid burnout.

There is a saying I thought I had made up, yet when I explored it I smiled to learn that it was famously said by a pioneer of the digital age, Steve Jobs.

The journey is the reward.

THANK YOU

Three years ago, if someone asked me if I thought I'd publish a book, I would have burst out laughting and called them crazy. Without doubt this has been one of the greatest challenges of my professional life and I hope it will be one of the most rewarding.

The reality is that, to make a project like this come to life, I had to slow down my fast-paced sales career, which if you haven't suspected by now, I am passionate about. Finding and interviewing 50 Elite salespeople, analysing the research, learning how to write a book, then writing a book and finally self-publishing is not a simple task. To commit to making this a reality, I paused my sales career. Towards the end of this project, with great pleasure, I stepped back in, which fuelled me.

There are several reasons and many people along the journey that kept me going to the point at which I can now write these words.

The first is you, the reader, the person who wants to better themselves and achieve all this career has to offer. I've been in your shoes and so have the 50 Elite salespeople I interviewed; we know the pain of establishing yourself and it's made even harder when there doesn't seem to be a clear route. My motivation to help people like you, and provide our career with a guide such as this, kept me on track.

For those who apply the knowledge within this book and further their careers to establish the lives they seek, I thank you even more. That is the purpose behind all of this.

My experiences alone are not enough to create such an in-depth view of an Elite sales career and then offer credible guidance. The 50 individuals who trusted in me to share their career stories, lessons and hardships so I could validate my hypothesis of how to build an Elite sales career, thank you. I thoroughly enjoyed getting to know every single one of you, and I admire your passion to help others succeed. Your encouragement kept me focussed on delivering what I set out to do.

There are some special mentions, first among all of those whom allowed me to share their stories within this book, in order of appearance:

1. Haig Hanessian, probably one of the hardest working people I've ever met.

2. Mandy Smithson, your energy rubs off on everyone you meet, I'm fortunate I had the opportunity to work with you at Salesforce.

3. Dan Czasnicki, a grafter with a purpose whom I've been fortunate enough to share numerous pints with.

4. Joachim Haas, the most extrovert German man I've met in my life. Your story has it all. A salesperson to his core and a humble gentleman, all in one.

5. Ben Tunstall, a man of grit and purpose. Thank you for your continued support and guidance throughout the creation of this book.

6. Steve Mason, your story truly shows it's not just about the money, it's about what makes you tick; may your story steer many to happiness, not just success.

7. Ben Jaderstrom, you reached Elite status faster than anyone I've met or interviewed and are always there to help others. Keep doing what you're doing, buddy!

8. Jon Levesque, one of the nicest guys I've met, I hope my writing brings out your personality, story and character. Your sales wisdom is something to share.

9. Marcus, textbook example of establishing the pillars and a man with limitless potential.

10. Brendan McLaughlin, at the latter part of his career, his story is a prime example of what truly matters and where to focus. It was an honour to get to know you Brendan, you taught me a lot.

11. Justin Golding, someone true to who they are and with wisdom beyond his years. Always a pleasure, Justin, may our paths cross again.

12. Phil Nyborg, your focus on how to be successful from a young age is an inspiration to all and your continued trajectory is one to watch.

13. Hugh Darvall, from an individual contributor to a VP of a region in several years at a large international tech company. Your words speak volumes and your actions, louder.

14. Suzanne McGettigan, your focus on success is unrivalled and is one thing that sets you apart. And I loved hearing your stories. They kept me on the edge of my seat!

15. Jefferson Mangus, a special thank you to you. I can't thank you enough for your regular check-ins to see my progress and offer support. It made the difference. It says a lot about you as a person, which I hope shines through in your story.

16. Ryan Chapman, how many stunt pilots do you meet in sales?? Your energy and no messing around attitude is your authentic self. Keep crushing it!

17. Madeleine Storr, your presence and approach commands respect in sales. I feel honoured to have worked alongside you at Salesforce and to see you grow as a professional.

34 out of the 50 Elite salespeople I interviewed gave me consent to share their stories and deciding who to include in the book was a very hard task. All provided inspiration and have stories to be told, so over time I will share their stories via my online content and I've no doubt their stories will be impactful to the reader/viewer.

A special mention to those 17 others: Ruairi Farrell, Neill Murphy, Stuart Waugh, Tim van der Hoeven, Adam Maris, Aleksander Bosnic, Anban Rajeswaran, Bryse Chandler, Christian Andersen, Cindy Taphoorn, Evert Hemelaar, Marco van London, Russell Henley, Tom Henshaw, Vala Shahabi, Wayne

Cheney, Wilco Flierman, and a special thanks to the 16 others who would rather remain unnamed.

PEOPLE WHO MADE
THE DIFFERENCE IN MY CAREER

To stumble across the idea for this book, I had to experience the journey of becoming an Elite salesperson: the hardships and the highs. There are several people who made a big difference along my path. In order of appearance:

1. Simon Kinsey, Managing Director of Sparkstone, my first full-time software sales job. Simon, thank you for giving me a chance and believing in my potential. Although I didn't achieve big success at your company, your teachings stayed with me.

2. Paul Thomas, Managing Director of Lead Forensics, your company taught me how to be a consistent top performer. Paul, you were the first inspirational person I met; I listened to every one of your motivational talks and applied your teachings. You taught me how to be the best.

3. Dean St John, a short-lived sales manager at Lead Forensics. Although Dean wasn't a company star, he encouraged me to take personal education seriously, which I did, and it played an enormous role in my success. Thank you, Dean, you may not realise how much of an impact this lesson had on my life.

4. Nick Spyer, previous General Manager of Salesforce Advertising EMEA. Despite my young age, you gave me a chance to join my dream company, which was single-handedly the biggest leap in my career. For sure, we both benefited from this decision! You were a friend as much as a mentor; it was a pleasure to have worked with you.

5. Daniel Pell, a high-performing senior sales leader at Salesforce. I've no doubt there is a long line of people to thank you Dan, for all that you do and the endless wisdom you share. You championed me at Salesforce, which elevated my status and played a large part in my success, thank you.

There are many more people who've coached me, advised me, and championed me throughout my sales career. I've always listened and I always will. Thank you to all of those people (the list is too long to start) and to all those future people I am to meet. Whether your impact on my success is big or small, I am grateful to all.

AUTHORS WHO HAVE INSPIRED ME

The desire to write a book and actually do it is because I know the difference a brilliant book has on one's career. There are several authors who made the difference to my career and are a source of inspiration for me to do the same:

1. Brian Tracy, one of the original and most successful authors on success. In chapter 2, I mention the difference you made to my career; when I read your book and applied the teachings of *The Psychology of Selling*, I doubled my income two years in a row. I have by now read four of your books. Thank you for everything that you do.

2. Jill Konrath, author of *Snap Selling*. Your book taught me to understand the prospects world and it instantly made a difference to gain mutual respect. To this day I use your teachings and rarely do I not gain mutual respect.

3. Neil Rackham, author of *SPIN Selling*. There is not a better method for identifying the cause of prospects' pain and quantifying the ROI of resolving it. SPIN is a skill I continue to refine and practise. Thank you for teaching the sales profession this valuable timeless knowledge.

4. Brent Adamson and Matthew Dixon, co-authors of *The Challenger Sale*. I love this approach to selling! It changes the conversation to a more innovative conversation, and this is how I sell. Thank you for bringing your teachings to the sales profession.

5. Simon Sinek, *Start with the Why*. A book I've read over three times, every time I find myself at a crossroads and I must refocus my path. When I know why I am doing something, my focus is clear. Thank you, Simon Sinek, for bringing this teaching to the world.

6. Malcolm Gladwell, multiple New York Times (NYT) bestseller. Your book *Outliers* inspired me and also your training videos of how to

become an author. Your style and knowledge to capture the reader is invaluable. We will find out how well I applied this! Thank you.

In my mind I have a library that you see in the films of old manor houses, which requires a ladder to reach the top shelf, while in reality my book collection will only fill one large bookcase, yet nonetheless, this is north of 100 books. Even though I buy most of my books digitally or listen to them via audiobooks, they symbolise my ever-growing knowledge of sales and life. The selection of authors listed are the ones who have made the biggest difference and thus caused this book to exist, yet there are many more who have made a big difference in my life. Thank you to every author out there who has a message to spread, which impacts lives, and who goes through the struggle to turn their idea into a book.

INDIVIDUALS WHO HELPED ME TURN THIS IDEA INTO A BOOK

Everyone above has contributed to the existence of this book, yet there are a few stand-out people who made the journey that much easier:

1. James Ski, Founder of Sales Confidence. There is not a single other person who championed my journey to becoming an author as much as you. When I told you what I was creating and why, you instantly bought into me. You got me up on stage to present my book to hundreds of salespeople and fast-tracked my traction. Thank you, James, for all that you do for the profession.

2. Ollie Sharpe, Chief Revenue Officer EMEA SalesLoft. You are a champion of the profession and helped by introducing me to a long list of people, several of whom feature in this book and influenced the creation. Thank you for your support and belief in my project.

3. Jasmin Naim, the editor of this book. You took the time to understand the meaning behind this book and put yourself in the shoes of the reader. Not only are your editing skills world-class, but the energy you bring to the table has made the process a lot of fun. Thank you for helping me turn my manuscript into a book ready for the big stage.

4. Alex Horton, the proof reader and arguably the second editor of this book. You finessed this book to ensure it stands shoulder to shoulder with the titans in the industry.

5. Mary Ann Smith, the book cover designer. It was a tough process finding the right design, but when we did everything instantly fell into place. You got it just right!

6. Steve Kuhn, the interior book designer. 1st design spot on, which is a rarity in creative work. Your quick turnaround and high quality of work has been much appreciated.

7. Dave Mohammed, the illustration designer. You brought my concepts to life in a way better than I pictured. May your work serve as a visual cue for the learning experience provided in this book.

MY CLOSEST AND DEAREST

Over the years, I've been fortunate enough to develop relationships with amazing people. My last thank you is to all of those people and they are my last thank you, because the creation of this book is only one area in life in which I'm fortunate enough to have them.

My immediate family, Mum, Guy (step-dad), Alex (brother) and Becki (sister), as dysfunctional a family as we can be, I know you support me and believe in me. This keeps me focussed and determined not to let you down.

My closest friends, almost all of whom laughed when I told them I was writing a book, but when they realised I was serious, did not doubt me for a second. Your friendship makes life ten times more fun and your belief in me keeps me focussed to do you proud.

Lastly, my girlfriend, life partner, the lady by my side every day, Axelle. When we first met, you thought I was writing a romantic novel set in the English countryside. Upon realisation that my book is about sales careers, you may have questioned your choice in me as your man. You tolerate my early mornings and late finishes to achieve what I set out to do. Our adventures and fun times keep life exciting. Our plans fuel me with motivation to win at life. Thank you for being the lady I want to be with.

If you've made it this far to read all my thank-yous, probably only Axelle to see her special mention, fair play...

The single purpose behind this book is to give those who seek to become successful in sales the blueprint to success. Now it is over to you. Go out there and be your best, work smart, work hard and enjoy life—it's only up from here.

My only ask is that you do something with this knowledge and if it helps you to succeed, share this book with others who want the same thing. We are all in this together!

REFERENCES

CHAPTER 1

1. U.S. Bureau of Labor Statistics (2020) *BLS Homepage*. https://www.bls.gov/ (Accessed 7 November 2020).

2. Smith, J. (2011) Companies that pay salespeople really well. *Forbes.com*. https://www.forbes.com/sites/jacquelynsmith/2011/05/20/10-companies-that-pay-salespeople-really-well/#4afb13324c9f (Accessed 7 November 2020).

3. Lambert, S. (2019) Who are the 1% and are you one of them? *This is money.com*. https://www.thisis-money.co.uk/money/comment/article-7357395/Who-1-Britain-one-them.html (Accessed 7 November 2020).

4. Wikipedia contributors (2020) Blockbuster LLC. *Wikipedia, The Free Encyclopedia*. https://en.wikipedia.org/w/index.php?title=Blockbuster_LLC&oldid=973675522 (Accessed 7 November 2020).

5. U.S. Bureau of Labor Statistics (2020) *Occupational Employment Statistics; 41-0000 Sales and Related Occupations (Major Group)*. https://www.bls.gov/oes/current/oes410000.htm (Accessed 7 November 2020).

6. The World Bank (2020) *Labor force, total—United States*. https://data.worldbank.org/indicator/SL.TLF.TOTL.IN?end=2019&locations=US&start=1990&view=chart (Accessed 7 November 2020).

7. Krogue, K., Larsen, G. & Parry, B. (2017) The State of Sales. *Insidesales.com*. https://uk.insidesales.com/wp-content/uploads//2017/09/State-of-Sales-9_15_17-Exec-Summary.pdf (Accessed 7 November 2020).

8. The World Bank (2020) *Labor force, total*. https://data.worldbank.org/indicator/SL.TLF.TOTL.IN (Accessed 7 November 2020).

9. Depersio, G. (2020) Why the British Pound is stronger than the U.S. Dollar. *Investopedia.com*. https://www.investopedia.com/ask/answers/070516/why-british-pound-stronger-us-dollar.asp#:~:text=For%20over%2020%20years%2C%20the,a%20low%20of%20approximately%201.23. (Accessed 7 November 2020).

CHAPTER 3

Gold Rush

1. Mannion, N. (2020) The Irish American who became the first millionaire west of the Mississippi. *The Irish Times*. https://www.irishtimes.com/life-and-style/abroad/the-irish-american-who-became-the-first-millionaire-west-of-the-mississippi-1.4254636 (Accessed 7 November 20).

2. Satanovsky, G. (n.d.) New York Herald publishes news of CA Gold Rush. *Famous Daily*. http://www.famousdaily.com/history/gold-rush-california-news-those-east-coast.html (Accessed 7 November 2020).

3. Yang, P. (2016) Miners vs Merchants: How global trade made men wealthy during the Californian Gold Rush. https://www.flexport.com/blog/trade-merchants-rich-california-gold-rush/ (Accessed 7 November 2020).

4. levistrauss.com (2020) *Levi's History*. https://www.levistrauss.com/levis-history/ (Accessed 7 November 2020).

The Rise of Technology

5. Johnston, S. (1997) Making the Arithmometer Count. *Bulletin of the Scientific Instrument Society*. 52, 21-21. https://www.mhs.ox.ac.uk/staff/saj/arithmometer/ (Accessed 7 November 2020).

6. mytypewriter.com (2020) Typewriter History. http://mytypewriter.com/explorelearn/ (Accessed 7 November 2020).

7. www.census.gov (2020) *The Hollerith Machine.* https://www.census.gov/history/www/innovations/technology/the_hollerith_tabulator.html (Accessed 7 November 2020).

8. Encyclopedia.com (2019) *Hollerith, Herman.* https://www.encyclopedia.com/education/economics-magazines/hollerith-herman (Accessed 7 November 2020).

9. Kidwell, P.A. (2000) The Adding Machine Fraternity at St. Louis: Creating a Center of Invention, 1880-1920 in *IEEE Annals of the History of Computing,* vol. 22, no. 02, pp. 4-21, 2000. https://doi.ieeecomputersociety.org/10.1109/85.841133 (Accessed 7 November 2020).

10. Early Office Museum (2016) *Adding and Listing Machines.* https://www.officemuseum.com/calculating_machines_adding_listing.htm (Accessed 7 November 2020).

11. IBM.com (2020) *IBM is Founded.* https://www.ibm.com/ibm/history/ibm100/us/en/icons/founded/ (Accessed 7 November 2020).

12. Deutsches Museum (2020) *The Enigma rotor cipher machine of the German Wehrmacht.* https://www.deutsches-museum.de/en/collections/meisterwerke/meisterwerke-ii/enigma/ (Accessed 8 November 2020).

13. The National Museum of Computing (2020) *The Turing-Welchman Bombe.* https://www.tnmoc.org/bombe (Accessed 8 November 2020).

14. Los Alamos National Laboratory (2013) *The history of computing from punched cards to petaflops.*

https://www.lanl.gov/discover/publications/national-security-science/2013-april/punched-cards-to-petaflops.php (Accessed 8 November 2020).

15. Deutsches Museum (2020) *The Z3 and Z4 of Konrad Zuse.* http://www.deutsches-museum.de/sammlungen/meisterwerke/meisterwerke-iii/z3-und-z4/ (Accessed 8 November 2020).

16. IBM (2020) *650 Applications. IBM Archives.* https://www.ibm.com/ibm/history/exhibits/650/650_ap1.html (Accessed 8 November 2020).

17. Cortada, J.W. (2019) Building the System/360 Mainframe nearly destroyed IBM. *IEEE Spectrum.* https://spectrum.ieee.org/tech-history/silicon-revolution/building-the-system360-mainframe-nearly-destroyed-ibm (Accessed 8 November 2020).

18. Orlicky, J. (1975) *Materials Requirement Planning.* McGraw-Hill.

19. Rashid, M.A., Hossain, L. & Patrick, J.D. (2002) The Evolution of ERP Systems: A historical perspective. https://faculty.biu.ac.il/~shnaidh/zooloo/nihul/evolution.pdf (Accessed 8 November 2020).

20. Oracle.com (2020) *What is ERP?* https://www.oracle.com/uk/applications/erp/what-is-erp.html (Accessed 8 November 2020).

21. Tout, N. (2009) The Calculator that spawned the microprocessor. *The International Calculator Collector.* http://www.vintagecalculators.com/html/busicom_141-pf_and_intel_4004.html (Accessed 8 November 2020).

22. Pollack, A. (1985) IBM and Microsoft join forces. *The New York Times.* https://www.nytimes.com/1985/08/22/business/microsoft-and-ibm-join-forces.html (Accessed 8 November 2020).

23. U.S. Department of Labor Statistics. (1999) *Computer Ownership up Sharply in the 1990s. Issues in Labor Statistics. Summary 4-99.* https://www.bls.gov/opub/btn/archive/computer-ownership-up-sharply-in-the-1990s.pdf (Accessed 8 November 2020).

24. ERP and more (2020) *About ERP History.* https://www.erpandmore.com/erp-reference/erp-history/ (Accessed 8 November 2020).

25. Waldrop, M. (2015) DARPA and the Internet Revolution. https://www.darpa.mil/attachments/(2015)%20Global%20Nav%20-%20About%20Us%20-%20History%20-%20Resources%20-%2050th%20-%20Internet%20(Approved).pdf (Accessed 8 November 2020).

26. CERN (2020) *The birth of the Web.* https://home.cern/science/computing/birth-web#:~:text=Tim%20

Berners%2DLee%2C%20a%20British,1989%2C%20while%20working%20at%20CERN. (Accessed 8 November 2020).

27. National Center for Supercomputing Applications (2020) *NCSA Mosaic™*. http://www.ncsa.illinois.edu/enabling/mosaic (Accessed 8 November 2020).

28. Hayes, A. (2019) Dotcom Bubble. *Investopedia*. https://www.investopedia.com/terms/d/dotcom-bubble.asp (Accessed 8 November 2020).

29. Davis, A. (2018) At one point, Amazon lost more than 90% of its value. But long-term investors still got rich. *CNBC.com*. https://www.cnbc.com/2018/12/18/dotcom-bubble-amazon-stock-lost-more-than-90percent-long-term-investors-still-got-rich.html (Accessed 8 November 2020).

30. Janeway, W.H. (2016) Enterprise Software: Death and transfiguration. *WTF?* https://wtfeconomy.com/enterprise-software-death-and-transfiguration-99eb1d3fc4c0 (Accessed 8 November 2020).

31. Cleveland, B. (2014) Lessons from the death of a tech Goliath. *Fortune.com*. https://fortune.com/2014/01/23/lessons-from-the-death-of-a-tech-goliath/ (Accessed 8 November 2020).

32. Dewey, C. (2016) 98 Personal data points that Facebook uses to target ads at you. *The Washington Post*. https://www.washingtonpost.com/news/the-intersect/wp/2016/08/19/98-personal-data-points-that-facebook-uses-to-target-ads-to-you/ (Accessed 8 November 2020).

33. Statista (2020) 2009—2019 annual revenue of Facebook. https://www.statista.com/statistics/268604/annual-revenue-of-facebook/

34. Apple Newsroom (2007) Apple reinvents the phone with iPhone. *Press Release*. https://www.apple.com/uk/newsroom/2007/01/09Apple-Reinvents-the-Phone-with-iPhone/ (Accessed 8 November 2020).

35. Broadband Search (2020) Mobile vs desktop internet usage statistics. https://www.broadbandsearch.net/blog/mobile-desktop-internet-usage-statistics

36. The Economist (2017) *The World's most valuable resource is no longer oil, but data*. https://www.economist.com/leaders/2017/05/06/the-worlds-most-valuable-resource-is-no-longer-oil-but-data (Accessed 8 November 2020).

37. GlobeNewswire (2010) *Flexera Software acquires Managesoft*. https://www.globenewswire.com/news-release/2010/05/04/1130927/0/en/Flexera-Software-Acquires-ManageSoft.html (Accessed 8 November 2020).

38. Gartner.com (2020) *Gartner Magic Quadrants*. https://www.gartner.com/en/research/methodologies/magic-quadrants-research (Accessed 8 November 2020).

39. Moore, G. (1991) *Crossing the Chasm*. Harper Business Essentials.

CHAPTER 4

1. Wikipedia contributors (2020) List of National Hockey League awards. *Wikipedia, The Free Encyclopedia*. https://en.wikipedia.org/w/index.php?title=List_of_National_Hockey_League_awards&oldid=968149287 (Accessed 8 November 2020).

2. MEDDIC Academy (2020) *MEDDIC sales methodology checklist*. https://meddic.academy/meddic-sales-methodology-checklist/ (Accessed 8 November 2020).

CHAPTER 5

1. Institute of Sales Management (2020) *History of the Institute of Sales Management*. https://www.ismprofessional.com/heritage/ (Accessed 8 November 2020).

2. Crawford, J.B. (2010) John Henry Patterson, Sales Pioneer. *Selling Power*. https://www.sellingpower.com/2010/02/02/3999/john-henry-patterson-sales-pioneer (Accessed 8 November 2020).

3. Barrett, S. (2020) The History of Sales Methodology—Part 1 (1900–1950s). *Head of Sales*. https://www.headofsales.com.au/2020/06/01/the-history-of-sales-methodology-part-2-1900s-1950s/ (Accessed 8 November 2020).

4. Carnegie, D. (1936) *How to Win Friends and Influence People.* Simon & Schuster. New York.

5. Bronten, G. (2016) A Brief History of Modern Sales Methodologies for Sales Leaders. *Membrain.* https://www.membrain.com/blog/a-brief-history-of-modern-sales-methodologies-for-sales-leaders (Accessed 8 November 2020).

6. Rackham, N. (1995) *SPIN Selling.* Gower Publishing.

7. Adamson, B. & Dixon, M. (2012) *The Challenger Sale.* Penguin Books.

8. Bryan, J. (2019) The Power of the Challenger Sales Model. *Gartner.com.* https://www.gartner.com/smarterwithgartner/power-challenger-sales-model/ (Accessed 8 November 2020).

9. Tracy. B. (2007) *The Art of Closing the Sale.* HarperCollins Leadership.

10. Ziglar, Z. (1982) *The Secrets of Closing the Sale.* Berkley Books.

11. Covey, S. (2004) *7 Habits of Highly Effective People.* Free Press. New York.

12. Sinek, S. (2009) *Start with the Why.* Portfolio. New York.

13. Clason, G.S. (1926) *The Richest Man in Babylon.* Penguin Books.

14. Robbins, T. (2017) *Unshakeable.* Simon & Schuster. New York.

CHAPTER 6

1. Saleh, K. (2019) Customer Acquisition vs Retention Costs—Statistics and Trends. *Invespcro.com.* https://www.invespcro.com/blog/customer-acquisition-retention/ (Accessed 8 November 2020).

CHAPTER 7

1. Mentorship (2020) In: *Cambridge English Dictionary* [online]. https://dictionary.cambridge.org/dictionary/english/mentorship (Accessed 8 November 2020).

2. Morgan, J. (2018) *What's it like to work at LinkedIn and how every company can create a lasting culture.* https://thefutureorganization.com/work-at-linkedin-every-company-lasting-culture/ (Accessed 8 November 2020).

3. The World Bank (2017) *Rapidly Assessing the Impact of Hurricane Matthew in Haiti.* https://www.worldbank.org/en/results/2017/10/20/rapidly-assessing-the-impact-of-hurricane-matthew-in-haiti (Accessed 8 November 2020).

4. Aircraftcompare.com (2020) *The Top 13 Fastest Fighter Jets in the World.* https://www.aircraftcompare.com/blog/fastest-fighter-jets/ (Accessed 8 November 2020).

5. Openview (2012) *ExactTarget IPO: Stock Price Soared 33.95% than Offering Price.* https://openview-partners.com/exacttarget-ipo-stock-price-soared-33-95-than-offering-price/#.Xz54LOhKjid (Accessed 8 November 2020).

6. Salesforce.com (2013) *Salesforce.com Signs Definitive Agreement to Acquire ExactTarget.* Press Release. https://www.salesforce.com/company/news-press/press-releases/2013/06/130604/ (Accessed 8 November 2020).

7. Adobe.com (2013) *Adobe Completes Acquisition of Neolane* Press Release. https://news.adobe.com/news/news-details/2013/Adobe-Completes-Acquisition-of-Neolane/default.aspx (Accessed 8 November 2020).

8. Oracle.com (2013) *Oracle buys Responsys.* Press Release. https://www.oracle.com/corporate/pressrelease/oracle-buys-responsys-122013.html (Accessed 8 November 2020).

9. Ha, A. (2015) Social media management company Sprinklr raises $46m, now valued at more than $1bn. *Techcrunch.com.* https://techcrunch.com/2015/03/31/sprinklr-joins-unicorn-club/?guccounter=1 (Accessed 8 November 2020).

CHAPTER 9

Muhammad Ali

1. Biography.com (2020) *Muhammad Ali Biography*. https://www.biography.com/athlete/muhammad-ali (Accessed 8 November 2020).

2. Thimmesch, N. & Parmiter, C. (1963) Muhammad Ali: The Dream. *Time Magazine*. https://time. com/3537815/muhammad-ali-dead-the-dream/ (Accessed 8 November 2020).

3. History.com (2018) *Muhammad Ali*. https://www.history.com/topics/black-history/muhammad-ali (Accessed 8 November 2020).

4. Anderson, D. (1971) Joe Frazier Beats Muhammad Ali in 'Fight of Century'. *The New York Times*. https://www.nytimes.com/2016/06/11/sports/joe-frazier-beats-muhammad-ali-in-fight-of-century.html (Accessed 8 November 2020).

5. Mitchell, K. (2015) Thrilla in Manila: 40 years on from sanctioned manslaughter in boxing. *The Guardian*. https://www.theguardian.com/sport/blog/2015/oct/01/thrilla-in-manila-40-years-on-muhammad-ali-joe-frazier-boxing (Accessed 8 November 2020).

6. Carbet, M. (2019) Oct. 30, 1974: Ali vs Foreman. *The Fight City*. https://www.thefightcity.com/ali-vs-foreman/ (Accessed 8 November 2020).

Roger Bannister

7. Hossain, A. (2014) Top 10 all-time individual achievements in sport. *Team Canada*. https://olympic. ca/2014/09/02/top-10-all-time-individual-achievements-in-sport/ (Accessed 8 November 2020).

8. New York Times (2018) *Roger Bannister, First Athlete to Break the 4-Minute Mile, Dies at 88.*

https://www.nytimes.com/2018/03/04/obituaries/roger-bannister-dead.html (Accessed 8 November 2020).

9. History.com (2020) *This Day in History: May 6, 1954: Roger Bannister runs first four-minute mile*. https:// www.history.com/this-day-in-history/first-four-minute-mile (Accessed 8 November 2020).

10. Chadband, I. (2018) The story of runner Roger Bannister, the 'Greatest Living Englishman'. *ESPN.com*. https://www.espn.com/sports/endurance/story/_/id/22677426/the-story-runner-roger-bannister-greatest-living-englishman (Accessed 8 November 2020).

11. McGowan, M. (2018) How Roger Bannister and John Landy raced to break the four-minute mile. *The Guardian*. https://www.theguardian.com/sport/2018/mar/05/how-roger-bannister-and-australian-john-landy-raced-to-break-the-four-minute-mile (Accessed 8 November 2020).

Bill Gates and Paul Allen

12. Elkins, K. (2019) Microsoft co-founders Bill Gates and Paul Allen got busted in high school for exploiting a bug in the computer system. *CNBC.com*. https://www.cnbc.com/2019/07/02/microsoft-co-founders-bill-gates-and-paul-allen-met-in-high-school.html (Accessed 8 November 2020).

13. Mejia, Z. (2018) Microsoft exists because Paul Allen and Bill Gates launched this high school business first. *CNBC.com*. https://www.cnbc.com/2018/10/16/microsoft-exists-because-paul-allen-and-bill-gates-launched-this-high-school-business.html (Accessed 8 November 2020).

14. Gates, B. (2019) The Side of Paul Allen I wish more people knew about. *GatesNotes.com*. https://www. gatesnotes.com/About-Bill-Gates/Forbes-Philanthropy-Summit-honors-Paul-Allen (Accessed 8 November 2020).

CHAPTER 10

1. World Health Organization (2019) Burn-out an "occupational phenomenon": International Classification of Diseases . https://www.who.int/mental_health/evidence/burn-out/en/ (Accessed 8 November 2020).

2. Wigert, B. & Agarwal, S. (2018) Employee Burn-out, Part 1: The 5 main causes. *www.gallup.com*. https://www.gallup.com/workplace/237059/employee-burnout-part-main-causes.aspx (Accessed 8 November 2020).

3. Wigert, B. (2020) Employee burn-out: the biggest myth. www.gallup.com. https://www.gallup.com/workplace/288539/employee-burnout-biggest-myth.aspx (Accessed 8 November 2020).

Printed in Great Britain
by Amazon

56471209R00122